# – Acknowledgements –

This book is dedicated to our many friends and staff that have contributed to the
Blueprint for Life study, whose efforts and contributions
have made this book possible.

First hardcover edition, January 2012

Printed in The United States.

10 9 8 7 6 5 4 3 2 1

For more information about Blueprint for Life, please visit blueprintforlife.com.

# BLUEPRINT FOR • LiFE.®

Michael Kendrick
& Ben Ortlip

**BLUEPRINT**
PUBLISHING

blueprintforlife.com

# BLUEPRINT FOR · LiFE®

# CONTENTS

*Chapter One*

# Your Personal Mission from God

"For we are God's handiwork, created in Christ Jesus to do good works, which God prepared in advance for us to do."

~ *Ephesians 2:10*

We love a story of destiny. Movies and books that portray an epic quest—a tale of how one person with a strong will and a lofty vision pursues an audacious goal and achieves it—it resonates with our hearts. We are drawn to unlikely heroes like Frodo Baggins, who overcomes impossible odds to rid the world of evil by casting a powerful ring into the fiery depths of the earth. Or of the legendary Arthur, whose dream was to build a Camelot based on noble virtues like equality and sacrifice. We marvel at the commitment of real-life people like "the Cambridge Seven," who gave up wealth and promising careers in 19th-century England to take the message of Jesus to obscure places in China. Or of biblical people like David, whose grand vision was to build a temple for God and follow His heart completely. Or of Paul, who endured remarkable suffering to take the gospel across the Roman Empire. We're even impressed by the worldly exploits of conquerors like Alexander the Great, who obsessively rise to heights of power at speeds we can scarcely imagine. Something about single-minded, wholehearted, big-picture adventures strikes a chord in the depths of our soul.

Why are we drawn to these stories? Because we were created to live one of them. Perhaps our story isn't as dramatic as the ones we see in a theater or read about in a biography, but it can certainly be just as important. We have a deep-down craving to live lives of significance, and God invites us to embrace that desire. We may not even realize we have it, perhaps because we got distracted somewhere along the way and decided our craving wasn't realistic. But it's still there. If we can find a way to be single-minded about it, to streamline our lives to accomplish one overriding purpose, our hearts will be satisfied.

> **We were designed to live out an epic story that takes us from beginning to end in order to accomplish something bigger than ourselves.**

The good news is that we can. We were designed to live out an epic story that takes us from beginning to end in order to accomplish something bigger than ourselves; worth living for. The problem for most of us is that we don't know how to get there. We need a little help to understand our purpose and discover how to accomplish it.

## THE QUESTIONS WE ASK

Why do you exist? Why are you here? What's the purpose of your life? Is it simply to have a good job and a good family and then retire somewhere on a beach or a golf course? Is that all there is? Isn't there more to our existence than decades of enduring the daily grind capped off by a few years of enjoying the breeze and hitting a little white ball in a hole? Isn't there a deeper meaning or a higher purpose?

If you're like most people, you've asked these kinds of questions. You've wondered why you seem to have a hole in your soul—a sense of emptiness, a longing for fulfillment, a deep desire for more in life. Perhaps you've wondered why this hole exists and why it seems so hard to fill. Maybe you've even resigned yourself to the void and assumed, like most people, that this is just the way life is—empty and unsatisfying. You may have seen a few glimpses of purpose and meaning along the way, but you've had a hard time understanding how your life fits the big picture. And those questions won't go away.

> **Every living person has a hole in their soul and, surprisingly, God strategically put it there.**

Every living person has a hole in their soul and, surprisingly, God strategically put it there. He made yours unique to you; it's carefully crafted by your Creator and unlike anyone else's. It's like a puzzle piece—exclusively designed to contribute to the big picture. This hole is a longing to do something that only you can do, and it's there because God wants to use it to draw you into His purposes. Your piece of the puzzle is a necessary part of the whole.

Until you carry out the mission God made you for, you'll be like a duck in the desert—always searching for someplace to use those feathers and webbed feet God gave you. God designed you with specific DNA and equipped you with specific gifts for a special purpose. He wants you to love and serve Him in a unique way. That's where the thirst in your soul comes from—you have gifts and abilities practically begging to be used in a meaningful way. This longing isn't meant to be a source of frustration. It's meant to propel you into God's purposes for your life. He fully intends to fill that hole.

If that's the case, all those questions about why we exist become a lot more specific. What's my mission? How can I find it? What do I do with it once I realize what it is? If God wants to fill that hole in my soul, why hasn't He? What do I have to do to find satisfaction and fulfillment in life? It's possible to discover the answers to all of these questions, but before we do, we need to understand a few things about God and why He created human beings in the first place.

## THE HEART BEHIND CREATION

God created this world out of nothing. He spoke, and it came into existence. His words are just that powerful. And the world He made was perfect—He declared it "good" in every phase of creation. It was intended to reflect His goodness and bring glory to Him.

After God had created the world and filled it with all kinds of living creatures, He made human beings in His image. Why would He want a creature made in His likeness? Because it's God's nature to love, and love is always sharing itself. God wanted to share Himself with beings who could relate to Him in their thoughts, their feelings, their attitudes, their will, their work, and in every other ability we can ascribe to God. When we love someone, we want to express our thoughts and feelings, to work together, and to enjoy each other. So does God. He created us with the capacity to relate to Him in all of these ways. He wants to know us and be known by us.

When we realize that this was the reason we were created, it changes everything. We begin to understand that God wants to share His goodness and display His wisdom, power, and love to everyone—in other words, to show His glory. We learn that He wants to be worshiped and adored; He is a jealous God who does not want us to put anything before Him in our lives. We realize we were created for Him—for His pleasure and His purposes. He enjoys interacting with us, and He invites us to know His heart and join Him in His work. When we respond to that invitation, we

> **So our primary purpose, the reason we were created, is to have a relationship with God.**

seek to please Him, serve Him, and glorify Him. This becomes the central focus of our lives.

So our primary purpose, the reason we were created, is to have a relationship with God. But that relationship involves much more than an occasional conversation with Him. We are not only meant to know Him, love Him, and glorify Him, we are also to partner with Him in accomplishing His purposes. His specific purposes include being glorified in the world, expanding His kingdom, and caring for the poor and downtrodden. In a nutshell, this means that His desire is to have an intimate relationship with us and then work with us and through us to establish a relationship with others who don't know Him.

## LONGING FOR A PURPOSE

That's the big picture, but what does it mean for you? How does that relate to why you sometimes feel empty, restless, and unfulfilled? Why would God let you work your way through life feeling unsatisfied and desperate? Why would He give you a hole in your soul?

God gives you a hole in your soul for the same reason that He made your stomach rumble when you get hungry: so you would eat. It's the same reason He made your nerves cause pain when you touch a hot stove: to keep you from burning yourself. God has built into us all kinds of uncomfortable senses to serve as warnings and signs that lead us into His good and perfect will for us. The yearning to know Him and accomplish His purposes is there for a very good reason. He lovingly placed a God-sized void in your heart so you would long for Him and pursue the mission He created you to fulfill.

If we don't understand this, we will never have complete peace and fulfillment in this world. In fact, we will spend a lot of time trying to fill that void with work and activities that don't satisfy. But if we do understand it and act on it, the

> **He lovingly placed a God-sized void in your heart so you would long for Him and pursue the mission He created you to fulfill.**

results can be amazing! The joy of knowing who you are, whom you were created for, and what you were created to do is indescribable.

So that's the first step on this journey: know that God created you for a unique purpose. No one else can carry out this purpose; it's designed specifically for you. Finding it is the key to discovering the peace, happiness, and joy you've been looking for. It's the only thing that will fill the hole in your soul.

That leads to an obvious question; how do you discover your unique mission? If it were easy to find, everyone would be walking in the joy of fulfilling their purpose. But most people are still living with a sense of emptiness, dissatisfaction and a lack of fulfillment. They may even know that they were designed for a unique purpose, but they aren't pursuing it because they don't know what it is. How can you find yours? That's what the rest of this book is about. We've talked about the big picture—God's overall purposes for this world and why He made human beings—and will look at that a little closer as we proceed. But His specific purpose for you is another matter. In the following pages, you'll begin a personal journey that will help you discover the unique mission God has called you to carry out.

## Three Big Risks

Before we discuss your unique design and calling, it may be helpful to know what's at stake if you don't find your mission from God. There are three huge risks in missing out on your calling in life:

1. *You can never have a fully developed and vibrant relationship with God.* That doesn't mean that you aren't a Christian or that His Spirit isn't living in you or hasn't spoken to you. You can have a genuine relationship with God regardless of whether you ever find your calling. You just can't experience a relationship that lives up to its highest purposes. You can't experience the fullness of what God wants you to experience.

Look at it like this: Imagine a husband and wife who are committed to each other and love each other deeply. Clearly, they can experience a genuine marriage relationship. But if they aren't on the same page in achieving their life's purposes, neither one of them is going to be totally fulfilled. There will always be a sense that something is missing. The partnership will be enough to make a home together, balance the checkbook, and raise kids, but if both partners aren't working together toward the same goals in life, something pretty important is missing.

Our relationship with God is like that. We can talk to Him, hear from Him, and enjoy the relationship up to a point, but if we aren't on the same page with His purposes for our lives, something will always be missing. We won't get to experience the partnership He designed us for. Like a premier athlete sitting on the sidelines or an eagle confined to a cage, we'll never get to use our gifts the way they were meant to be

> **If you aren't on the same page with His purposes for our lives, something will always be missing.**

used. He will still meet our needs and help us grow, but we won't reach our potential.

*2. You will miss out on an amazing joy-filled life that God specifically prepared for you to experience.* There's no greater joy than to know you are living in your "sweet spot" with your Creator. When your heart is centered on Him and you are pursuing the purpose He has for you, you can sense God's pleasure. He will have you drink from the fountain of "living water" that quenches the thirst He placed on your tongue when He created you. Jesus invites you into a relationship with Him not just so you can carry out His will but so you can be full of joy (John 15:11). And that relationship includes partnering with Him in His purposes according to your unique calling. Your mission in life brings joy to you and those around you.

> **God will have you drink from the fountain of "living water" that quenches the thirst He placed on your tongue when He created you.**

*3. Your eternal future depends on it! You are an everlasting being. Your life will never end.* Your body—your "earth suit"—will wear out, and one day you will slip it off like a pair of pajamas in the morning. Every person God created will live forever, either in paradise with Him or in darkness separated from His presence. Our salvation, which we can only receive by placing our faith in Jesus as our Savior, ensures that we will live with Him forever. But the Bible is also very clear that we will be rewarded based on how well we accomplished the mission He has given us. The ways we handle our time, our resources, our gifts, our talents, our opportunities, and our relationships all have an impact on the life we experience in eternity. We don't know exactly how that works—what God will use

> **The waking hours we have each day become a fulcrum by which we can leverage all of eternity.**

as rewards or how our spiritual fruit on earth will be manifested in heaven—but we do know that Jesus spoke of rewards often. Eternal riches are a reality. The waking hours we have each day become a fulcrum by which we can leverage all of eternity. There is a direct connection between what you do today and what you will experience in eternity. That's amazing! There is no better opportunity for a greater investment. We can sow seeds now that will bear fruit forever. So we must always ask ourselves what we are doing today that has value in eternity. If your actions today do have the potential to radically effect your eternity, wouldn't that dramatically change how you think about your life?

## A VISION FOR LIFE

By now, you may be thinking: "Great. I can have an amazing, joyful, God-sized adventure on earth and store up treasure in heaven—IF I know what my mission from God is. That makes not knowing even more frustrating!" But don't get frustrated yet; we're getting there. God won't hide your calling from you. He will lead you into His purposes. As we prepare for this journey, begin asking yourself a few questions:

- If life gave you exactly what you asked for, what would it be like?

- If you could paint a life portrait in vivid detail, what would it look like?

- Do you live reactively, responding to anything that comes your way? Or are you looking through a carefully designed grid so you can accept only those things that support your vision for the future and filter out whatever doesn't?

• Are you developing a clear picture of God's call for your life? Do you know what He has uniquely designed you for and equipped you to accomplish?

This last question is the subject of the rest of this book. Vision is important. In fact, vision is the dominant factor that governs your life. The Bible speaks often of the need for vision and assures us that God will give us the direction we need. He will not let us wander aimlessly, even when life seems to be taking us in random directions. God's Word clearly illustrates that He leads His people and gives them promises of the future He has called them to fulfill. Those who have followed Him have found Him faithful. They have grown closer to Him as they partner with Him to do His will. They eventually accomplish the mission He has given them. And they experience the joy and satisfaction of doing exactly what they were created to do.

That can be your story too. In the pages to come, we will share with you how to evaluate your skills, gifts, and passions and how to combine those into a vision for your future that will allow you to live out your unique mission given by your Creator. If you've been searching for purpose—if that hole in your soul has been longing to be filled—this may be a huge turning point in your life. You can discover the life you were born to live.

> **If you've been searching for purpose—if that hole in your soul has been longing to be filled—this may be a huge turning point in your life.**

BLUEPRINT
FOR •
L*i*FE.

*Chapter Two*

# The Meaning of Life

"Strange is our situation here upon earth. Each of us comes for a short visit, not knowing why, yet sometimes seeming to divine a purpose."

~ *Albert Einstein*

On July 21, 1969, Neil Armstrong and Buzz Aldrin became the first human beings to set foot on the moon. For most observers, it was a dream they had heard about for years and then watched on TV as the dream was finally fulfilled. But for those who had a hand in this major accomplishment, it was a long, dedicated process. What was involved? Decades of technological developments. Years of training for the people involved. A thoroughly mapped-out agenda called the Apollo Program. Extensive funding. Incredibly complex designs and calculations that accounted for physical forces like gravity, rotation and orbits of heavenly bodies, weights and measures, exact timing, fuel and engines, support systems, supply systems, communication systems, data processing, and more. In other words, it wasn't a whim or a happy accident. It was a long process of thorough planning and total dedication.

That's how the most worthwhile and ambitious goals are fulfilled. They don't just happen. Our life's journey doesn't randomly put us where we need to be. Our resources don't just coincidentally line up to support our agendas. In order to accomplish anything significant, there needs to be plans. If we want to get from point A to point B in life, we need to identify point B and figure out a way to get there. We have to be intentional about it. Ask yourself, what do you want your life to become, develop details and a plan and then focus on it.

## THE IRRESISTIBLE PULL

> **Ask yourself, what do you want your life to become, develop details and a plan and then focus on it.**

For many people, life is a compromise of a God-given dream. It may not be a complete disappointment, but there's a haunting feeling that it is meant to be so much more. And in every case, our compromises can be traced directly to a lack of purpose somewhere in our lives. We don't quite see how the pieces should fit together, so we don't pursue the whole puzzle. We celebrate a career accomplishment here or a family milestone there, but when it comes to an overall sense of meaning, our existence remains an enigma. Meanwhile, our souls constantly cry out for the fulfillment of those things God placed in our hearts to accomplish.

Isn't it true that if we truly understood why we're here, our lives would look completely different? That is, if we laid hold of our purpose and worked out what it should look like in each arena of life, the impact would be stunning. Suddenly, the things we quietly long for—the God-born passions of our heart—would move front and center and become our uncompromising focus. We would instantly have the courage to let go of all the benign activities that fill up our days and weeks and lives with busyness. That's what lies in store for those who are willing to plan their life around their God-given purpose.

God doesn't give us a crystal ball to see our future, so we can't plan out all the details. Only He has the right to plan our lives, so we certainly aren't talking about mapping everything out and controlling our future.

But if we understand our purpose and the calling God has given us, we can filter every opportunity and decision through that understanding. When something comes along that fits our God-given purpose, we can ask if He wants us to pursue it. When something comes along that doesn't fit that purpose, we can know that it isn't His will. As we interact with Him in this process, our relationship with Him will grow. In an ongoing conversation with Him, we can develop a blueprint for our life.

That may sound like this is a book on setting goals and making plans, but that doesn't get at the heart of who you are. Many people spend their lives straining to get ahead—with a plan—but still don't know exactly where they are going or why they are going there. They just want to reach their potential—whatever it happens to be. So they push forward. But without knowing their real purpose, they are always running forward yet never quite getting where they want to be. They end up overextended—maxed out and burned out.

The truth is that you don't have to max out in your life to reach your full potential. Finding our unique mission isn't just about doing more or about setting goals and reaching them. It's about tapping into the deepest longings of your heart—longings your Creator put within you in the first place.

> **You were not designed by your Creator to push yourself through life but to be pulled by something compelling and irresistible.**

You were not designed by your Creator to push yourself through life but to be pulled by something so compelling and irresistible that there would be an empty space inside if you didn't follow. That irresistible something—that deep-down desire that you sometimes can't even put your finger on—is your purpose in life. This God-given purpose is the purest source of direction. Sermons and Bible studies can teach you about Christian principles in general, but that won't be enough to guide you personally and specifically. Only your purpose reveals the unique plans God laid out for your life when He created you.

Life is about fulfilling the unique purposes you were created to accomplish in God's universe. In order to do that, you'll need to know what your unique purposes

> **Life is about fulfilling the unique purposes you were created to accomplish in God's universe.**

are and then pursue them very intentionally. That requires making a plan that reflects who you are at your core and is based on the way God designed you—or, as we like to call it, creating a blueprint for your life.

This is a process, of course. You don't just do it once and consider yourself done with it. Planning your life is an ongoing channel of communication between you and God, a conversation with Him in which you discover who you are and why you're here. It's important to remember that this planning process is not simply about finding the right assignment, as though God were only interested in hiring workers for a job or drafting volunteers to carry out His agenda. Our purpose in life is primarily relational, not task-oriented. He wants to be known. But in the context of a deep relationship with Him, we discover our purpose and calling. Our assignment grows out of an intimate connection with His heart. So your process of developing a blueprint really is a conversation, one in which you'll grow closer to Him along the way. And it's perhaps the most important conversation of your life.

## FROM PURPOSE TO PLAN

Why do you need a Blueprint for Life? Well, maybe you've probed into God's purpose for your life before. Perhaps you've begun to understand your unique wiring, your strengths and weaknesses, and your passions. You may have even scripted a life-purpose statement or a personal mission. But here's the watershed question: *Has exploring your purpose served any purpose?* In other words, has your understanding of your purpose in life changed the way you actually live? Or has it simply tweaked the perspective from which you live the life you were already living?

> **Has exploring your purpose served any purpose? In other words, has your understanding of your purpose in life changed the way you actually live?**

It's one thing to have an inner peace that the road you're on is going somewhere—that there is a purpose and there is meaning. That's a good start. But purpose without plans is purposeless. When you truly grasp God's calling on your life—for every area of your life—it will show up on your calendar, in your checkbook ledger, and in your decision-making. The choices you make will reflect the calling you have been given.

That's why you need a blueprint. It will help you align your choices with your calling and live with the assurance that you're in sync with God's will. With that kind of clarity, you won't have to drag yourself out of bed in the morning. You'll begin each day energized by the mission you were designed to fulfill.

## DEVELOPING A BLUEPRINT

A blueprint is a rough draft—a picture of the end product as seen by the architect. With a Blueprint for Life, you suddenly know where to turn for reference when making key decisions. There are written plans to help you recognize when things are on track and when it's time to take the next step in life. There is guidance for establishing a strong foundation, developing your inner wiring, even tending to the cosmetic details. When the house is built according to the plans, it will fulfill every purpose your Architect intended.

Your Blueprint for Life goes far beyond simply learning your calling and purpose. It includes a plan for intentional living in every area of life. But most importantly, it approaches these details from the perspective of eternity. There's something empty about setting new career goals, or saving for a new car, or planning for retirement. When they're over, they're over. But when you place those things in the context of a life blueprint that includes eternity, it changes everything. Suddenly, your career becomes a catalyst in support of your life's mission. Your home, car and personal possessions suddenly take on a new role as tools to support your life's mission. And your golden years become a key stage of life on your journey toward your purpose in God. But unless you see how your life goals support the eternal quest God has placed inside you, they will always bear overtones of futility.

> **Your Blueprint for Life goes far beyond simply learning your calling and purpose. It includes a plan for intentional living in every area of life.**

A life blueprint gives you a practical framework for life. It is a set of plans to organize your life's priorities and determine specific action steps to make sure you meet the objectives that will create a true sense of fulfillment—right now, in the coming years, and forever.

## A PLACE TO THINK ABOUT YOUR LIFE

You've probably had glimpses throughout your life of where God is leading you. It's not that you have no ideas about His plan, but maybe you need some clarity when it comes to the details—something you can cling to as a reminder of where you're going, and why. After all, if you're like most people, you've never written those glimpses down. And even if you have, how do you use that information to help you fulfill the specific dreams God has given you—whether it's the second honeymoon you promised yourself, spending quality time with your aging parents, or finally developing your latent musical talent? You owe it to yourself to determine which of those dreams are part of God's plan for your life and then to develop a plan to make them happen. Good intentions without written plans are like ships without rudders. It's just a matter of time before we drift.

> **Good intentions without written plans are like ships without rudders. It's just a matter of time before we drift.**

That's where your life blueprint comes in. God wants His people to know what He's up to. He has communicated His overarching plans for things like salvation, the nation of Israel, the church, and heaven, but His will gets much more personal than that. The only way for you to get to know Him and work with Him is for you to know the plan He has for your life. That includes discovering the kingdom assignments He has prepared for you as well as enjoying the pleasures He has placed in your heart—

Does your heart leap when thinking about adopting a child? Do you have a deep sense of satisfaction when helping the poor? Perhaps taking trips to countries you've never been to? All of it is part of a plan to live a life shaped by your close relationship with Him. Blueprint for Life is your chance to take out a piece of paper and say, "Lord, I'm listening and I'm taking notes. Tell me everything you want me to know."

Please don't misunderstand. The path to the destiny God has planned for you may not be a straight one. In fact, it probably won't be. There are twists and turns we can't plan for, delays that may seem designed to frustrate us, and directions God will reveal to us later that He won't divulge today. This is the way it was for most of the great Bible characters God used in powerful ways. Abraham had to wait 25 years for the promise of a son to be fulfilled. Joseph got a blueprint of his destiny in a dream, and for more than a decade afterward, his life seemed to be going in exactly the opposite direction. Moses tried to fulfill his calling as a deliverer and then spent the next 40 years in exile until the timing was right and he was fully prepared. David knew he was called to be king but had to flee from an enraged King Saul for years before his blueprint ever began to materialize. God has preparation processes that we simply can't map out, and sometimes those processes take a really long time. They can be extremely frustrating too, especially when we know our calling and, for whatever reason, can't get there. God may show us our purpose but allow the doors of opportunity to be closed for years. We can't plan everything out.

But the point of having a blueprint isn't to plan everything out anyway. It's to have a grid for the decisions we make and, as much as it's up to us, stay on track with the calling God has given us. We must submit to His processes and His timing, but in the meantime, we can avoid making conflicting choices or getting involved in distracting pursuits that will only prolong the processes even further. It's our responsibility to be ready to move forward in His timing with the mission He has given us. The best way to prepare for that is to have a blueprint in mind—to know our calling and to be intentional about the way we invest our time, resources, and relationships in pursuing it.

So it's important to remember that discovering your purpose in life is an ongoing process. It will likely evolve and change as you complete each phase of life and receive the next assignment. There's nothing wrong with adapting it. Resist the idea that revising your purpose means you were wrong in the first place. It only means you didn't have all the information at the time. So don't feel that if you're specific about it now, you're limiting yourself. Try to develop your blueprint as clearly as you can based on what you know right now. And that begins with asking some fundamental questions about your life.

## WHO AM I?

Every blueprint begins with a clear understanding of the building's purpose. The design should reflect the reasons for which it is built. Your life blueprint is no different. If you're going to live the rest of your life meaningfully, it's vital to understand as much as you can about why you exist.

> You'll never grasp the full meaning of your life apart from the context of what God is up to in the world.

In the first chapter, we discussed the reason human beings were created. That's important to know because you'll never grasp the full meaning of your life apart from the context of what God is up to in the world. Some purposes—like worshiping God, glorifying Him, and joining Him in His kingdom's mission—are common to all human beings. But if you're like most people, the question you really want an answer for is specifically why you were created. After all, you were God's idea, so you are defined in Him. You exist because of some specific intention He has in mind. So there's an unbreakable link between His purpose and yours.

This is huge. It's a common mistake to seek a purpose in life—apart from knowing why God created you and knowing His purpose. As God's creation, you are incomplete without *His* purpose. Not just any purpose, but the particular purpose He has for you. So you must first recognize that it's not really your purpose you seek—it's God's purpose for you. Knowing your purpose gives meaning to your life. Without purpose life has no meaning. The greatest tragedy is not death, but a life without purpose.

> **As God's creation, you are incomplete without His purpose. Not just any purpose, but the particular purpose He has for you.**

Naturally, His purpose for you specifically is going to fit with His overall purpose for the world. To discover the way for yourself, you must first discover something about God's ways. The better you recognize God's agenda, the better you can envision a valid agenda for your own life. Following your own purposes will be like trying to sail against the wind, but when you pursue God's purpose, you sail with the current. The forces of the universe are at His fingertips, so as you follow His will, you'll find the universe bending to accommodate your quest. That doesn't mean there will be no obstacles along the way, but when God writes the story, the protagonist always succeeds in the end.

## What in the World Is God Doing?

We begin by observing what God is up to in our world, and then we begin to form a basic direction for our lives. For example, if God is restoring the world to Himself through love, we can't expect to find long-term fulfillment in something that doesn't serve that goal. If one of His specific instructions is to "make disciples," then we're more likely to be satisfied when something about our lives supports that effort or one of His other stated purposes. That doesn't mean that everyone would be most fulfilled as an evangelist on the mission field, of course. But our natural skills and abilities will find their maximum meaning in the context of accomplishing God's purposes around the world.

Sometimes the connection between our efforts and God's purpose is indirect—setting aside some income to feed the hungry, offering skills and services to organizations that support God's interests, even taking a job that seems on the surface to be a low priority but that positions us to serve and minister to the people around us can give us complete meaning in life. And this extends well beyond career roles. We're also a husband or wife, father or mother, brother or sister, friend, neighbor, community volunteer, and more. Each of these areas of life is an opportunity from God, and each comes with a responsibility to consider the reason He gave that opportunity. But whether our many and varied connections to God's interests are direct or indirect, our participation in His plan is just as real and valid.

So a person's purpose in life is more accurately described as a set of purposes. Some might say Moses' purpose was to lead Israel out of Egypt to the Promised Land, or that Christopher Columbus' was to discover America, or that the Wright brothers' was to pioneer modern aviation. But if you asked those people to summarize their purpose in life, their answers may not be so simple. The truth is that we all serve many purposes in God's plan. Abraham Lincoln led America away from the practice of slavery, but he was also a son who honored his parents, a husband who loved his wife, and a father who trained his sons. So avoid the temptation to sum up your purpose as a single, landmark accomplishment. Your purposes in life, reflected in the roles you play, are many.

The ultimate sense of purpose comes when your primary talents converge in the performance of some vital function in God's plan. When all the different roles in your life align around a primary purpose, the impact is more profound. And only when that purpose belongs to

> **The ultimate sense of purpose comes when your primary talents converge in the performance of some vital function in God's plan.**

God will there be lasting satisfaction. Once you begin to identify how God wants to use you—your purpose in life—you will see ways to work along with Him to maximize your impact in accomplishing His agenda. This is a landmark point in a person's self-understanding and relationship with God. When you move from an unwitting creation of God to an intentional servant of God, life takes on new dimension. Suddenly, you embark in a partnership with the Creator of the universe. What could be more meaningful than that?

## WHY AM I HERE?

So far, we've established two important points. First, your purpose is contained in God's purpose. Second, your purpose is really defined as a set of purposes. That helps narrow it down, but it doesn't exactly answer

> **When you move from an unwitting creation of God to an intentional servant of God, life takes on new dimension.**

the question of your specific purpose. You may still be wondering, "So why am I here?"

The good news is that your purpose is not obscured in lofty, spiritual secrecy. It's written all over you. It's in the fingerprint of God stamped into your life when you were created. It emanates from your being with every breath you take. Even though we all have a sinful nature, we were nevertheless made in the image and likeness of God. By nature, therefore, we are each a unique reflection of His desires and plans. Like individual fingerprints, we each form a vital stroke in the master blueprint for the universe. Discovering your purpose is quite simply a matter of examining His fingerprint on your soul.

Paul wrote that we are "God's workmanship, created in Christ Jesus for good works, which God prepared beforehand, that we should walk in them" (Ephesians 2:10). That means God was thinking about the blueprint for your life long before you were born. He created you for good works. But more than that, God has prepared many of your appointments in life personally, *beforehand*. All you have to do is "walk in them."

The picture here is of someone stepping onto the stage and simply following a script that God has written. Imagine that. God has been preparing in advance for thousands or perhaps millions of years in anticipation of your life. And He has reserved certain good works just for you. No one else can do them. All you have to do is walk in the path He has laid out for you.

So if your purpose is written all over you, it follows that you can begin to discover it by asking yourself a few basic questions. What are you

really good at? What do you do effortlessly? What do some people have to toil
at that you find easy and enjoyable to do?
What kinds of things do people ask for
your help with? These kinds of questions
explore your skills and abilities, which
are a huge indication of what God has
designed you to do.

> **Discovering your purpose is quite simply a matter of examining His fingerprint on your soul.**

In addition, you'll need to ask some questions that explore your desires.
What do you have a passion for? What do you really enjoy? What kind
of work do you find rewarding? What do you gravitate toward when you
have some extra time? What activities cause you to feel like time is flying
by? Identifying the desires of your heart will also give you a clue to your
unique design.

Your combination of skills, gifts, passions, and personality is unlike anyone else's on earth. If you can answer the questions in the previous two
paragraphs, you probably already have some idea of what God has created
you to do. There may be some specifics that you don't know yet—gifts
and passions can be applied in many different ways, depending on the opportunities God gives you—but you can at least have a general idea of the
nature of your mission. There's a reason you have the gifts and passions you
have. God didn't equip you with traits and abilities that conflict with His
purposes. He designed you very intentionally and specifically.

We can diagram this design in something we call the Life Impact Triangle:

**What Accomplishes God's Purposes**

**What You Are Highly Skilled at Doing
(Your Giftedness)**

**What You Really Love Doing
(Your Passions)**

This diagram shows your areas of giftedness and your passions at the bottom of the triangle, and both serve to point toward God's purposes at the top of the triangle. The way they all work together determines the impact your life can have for God and His kingdom. The more these three points work in harmony, the greater the impact—and the greater your level of fulfillment in life.

Think about that. Isn't that what everyone wants—fulfillment? A life that's full of joy, peace, contentment, and meaning? Many people are constantly striving for this kind of life and always falling short of it. They unwittingly fill their lives with things that don't really satisfy in the long run and don't really point them in the right direction. They end up with a lot of activity, a lot of clutter in their schedules, and a lot of substitutes for fulfillment. Some feel like they are wandering aimlessly, and some feel constantly overextended because they've pursued

> **There's a reason you have the gifts and passions you have.**

too many opportunities. Why? Because they don't understand how their gifts and passions work together to fit their unique design and to serve God's purposes.

It really is possible to leap out of bed each day with clarity of purpose, knowing that you are in harmony with what your Creator designed you to do. You can know that you are pleasing Him and be filled with unimaginable joy as you pursue the destiny He has ordained for you. That doesn't mean you'll never have bad days or struggle with the trials and tribulations of life. But it does mean you can face them with confidence that you are headed in the right direction and fulfilling your purpose. And, in the process, God is crediting your heavenly account with eternal rewards that we can't even begin to understand.

> **It really is possible to leap out of bed each day with clarity of purpose, knowing that you are in harmony with what your Creator designed you to do.**

This is why we need to stop thinking of eternal life as something far off in the mystical future. Eternal life is right now. It begins when we accept Christ as our Savior, and we experience it very practically when we grab hold of the mission we've been given and pursue it. That's what we were created for—not just eternal life one day in heaven, but eternal life as a reality today. We all have major shortcomings and weaknesses, but when we look in the mirror, we need to see ourselves as God sees us—His workmanship, perfectly created in His image and redeemed for His purposes. All we need to do is clear our eyes and see the vision He has for us.

Can you see His vision for you? Do you know what your Life Impact

Triangle looks like? If you want to see your life's mission with crystal clarity, read on. The following chapters will help you bring it into greater focus.

*Chapter Three*

# God's Blueprint for Success

"Success is not what you've done compared to what others have done. Success is what you have done compared to what you were supposed to do."

~ *Tony Evans*

We live in a world that tells us constantly what's important and what we ought to be striving for. It promises that we can have a fulfilling life if we hang out with the right people, drive the right car, wear the right clothes, drink the right beer, find security in the right insurance, exude the right scent, and on and on and on. But what if we strive after this kind of life and find out later that we were really being measured by other criteria? What if we're competing with one set of standards in mind while another set of standards is much more important? What if we're pursuing the wrong things?

That's the dilemma we find ourselves in. We wrestle with conflicting value systems, often completely unaware that we're doing so. We mentally envision the lifestyle we desire and then subconsciously do everything we can to step into that vision. Sometimes we make progress, and sometimes we get frustrated. But sometimes we just need to ask ourselves if it's even the right vision to begin with. We need to pursue what really matters.

## God's Value System

Have you ever noticed that God's value system is radically different from ours? Think about what His Word tells us: In His kingdom, the first will be last and the last will be first. In order to be great in His kingdom, we must become servants. The proud will be humbled, but the humble will be exalted. Those who mourn are the ones who are truly happy.

> **Have you ever noticed that God's value system is radically different from ours?**

Only when we become weak are we in a position to be experience His strength. And in order to truly live, we must die to ourselves.

These are some of the many paradoxes in scripture—attitudes and actions that surprisingly reflect God's values and lead to our fulfillment. On the surface, it looks to us like His value system is completely backwards. Of course, He isn't backwards at all; we're the ones who need to be reoriented to what's really true. For example, we wouldn't think radical obedience to God really leads to freedom, but it does. We wouldn't expect that the "least" members of our society are often the greatest in God's kingdom, but they are. So it really shouldn't surprise us that God defines success entirely differently than we do. He uses very different measures.

The world defines success by looking at things like status, income, achievements, accolades, and job titles. We admire stars like Johnny Depp and Angelina Jolie and Beyoncé for their successful careers. We marvel at innovators like Bill Gates and Steve Jobs for their successful ingenuity. We envy business magnates like Warren Buffet and Ted Turner for their successful bank accounts and net worth. The list could go on and on—star athletes, famous TV personalities, powerful political leaders. Whether we like these people or not, we call them "successful" because they have money, fame, or power. But these people might not be successful at all—by God's definition. He doesn't consider the CEO of a Fortune 500 company

> **Success is not what you've done compared to what others have done. Success is what you have done compared to what you were supposed to do.**
> **- Tony Evans**

to be a success simply because of his or her position. A $120,000 Mercedes or a 10,000-square-foot mansion doesn't impress Him. He doesn't care if we make a name for ourselves and get interviewed by Oprah. He sees things differently.

In His value system, successful people are those who do with excellence the things He calls them to do. We can't measure our success by comparing ourselves to others; the issue is whether we accomplish our God-given assignment and do what we were designed to do. Success is not what you've done compared to what others have done. Success is what you have done compared to what you were supposed to do. This concept of true success is difficult for us to understand because we're so used to measuring people by visible signs of success like money, power, fame, beauty, and material possessions. This is the world's perspective, and it's contrary to God's. It's possible to have all of those measures in abundance and still be a failure. Money and power can easily be lost, beauty fades, and fame is fickle. All the trappings of success can come and go quickly and easily. But God values the impact of our lives.

God measures inward growth and outward fruitfulness, often in ways we can't even see. His ways are not our ways and His thoughts are not our thoughts (Isaiah 55:8-9). Even His simplest truths confound the wise (Luke 10:21; 1 Corinthians 1:25). When He delivered His people from Egypt, He chose methods and pathways that looked ill-informed and even disastrous at first but led to decisive victory in the end. When He sent the prophet Samuel to anoint a new king, He told him not to look at outward appearances because God looks at the heart (1 Samuel 16:7). In choosing His prophets, He often selected people whose status or appearance was unappealing but whose message was pure. He seems to enjoy choosing the least likely candidates for success—the foolish, the weak, and the uneducated—and making them experts in His ways.

Perhaps the best illustration of God's perspective on success is His own Son. Jesus wasn't born into a wealthy family with a lot of earthly fanfare. He was born in a stable among farm animals and placed in a manger. He grew up in the family of a hard-working carpenter in a normal town in an out-of-the-way region of the empire. When it came time to choose which of His followers He would train, He didn't select well-educated scholars, decorated military leaders, or astute businessmen. He chose rough, common fishermen, a despised tax collector, and other ordinary guys. When His reputation grew to the point that people were ready to crown Him as their leader, He allowed Himself to be executed by one of the most humiliating and disgraceful instruments of torture ever devised. He died in a way most people considered shameful.

In spite of His humble beginnings and shameful death, Jesus was amazingly successful. Why? Because He completed all that His Father sent Him to do (John 17:4). None of us would have designed a plan for the Savior of the world to come and die; this isn't our normal vision for

> **Success is completing with excellence the mission that God has specifically called you to accomplish.**

success. But, as we've seen, God's value system is not at all like ours. His conditions for success involve attitudes and actions that reflect His character and that accomplish His purposes. His grand strategy emphasizes humility and sacrifice, not wealth and fame and beauty. He doesn't measure our success by how we compare to others. He measures it by how well we fulfill our calling.

So as we try to discern our life impact and plan for success, we'll probably need to think a little differently than we normally do. We'll have to go against our natural inclinations and envision a kind of success that's more meaningful and more lasting. The question isn't "What does success look like?" It's much more specific: "In light of God's values and my calling, what does success look like for me?"

## POSITIONED FOR SUCCESS

Think about it: If God has a mission in mind for you, something He specifically created for you to fulfill, then He would give you the right tools for the assignment. Psalm 139 tells us that He knows everything about us; He even knit us together in our mother's womb. He ordained all our days before we ever began to live them. So with knowledge that detailed and personal, He clearly would give you the necessary gifts and skills to make you very effective in your mission. Not only that, He would give you the right fuel to help you go the distance. This fuel is called "passion." We may not be born with it, but time and experience have a way of cultivating our passions and focusing them in certain directions. God instills these passions in us in order to point us toward our calling and motivate us to accomplish it. So if we want to understand our mission, we can get a pretty clear picture by looking at our gifts, skills, and passions.

> So if we want to understand our mission, we can get a pretty clear picture by looking at our gifts, skills, and passions.

That's what the Life Impact triangle

in the last chapter was about. The two points at the base of the triangle were your skills and passions, and the peak of the triangle was God's purposes. That diagram represents how the puzzle pieces of someone's life can fit together to create a purposeful whole. But we're not just talking about someone's life, are we? We're talking about yours. And when you start to fill in those blanks with your specific skills and passions, an exciting picture begins to emerge.

So let's engage in a fun exercise to discover the mission God has created you to accomplish. What did He have in mind for you from the beginning when He designed you? Well, you can answer that question by asking some others. What do you love to do? What activities do you really enjoy? Are you an outdoors person, or do you thrive in an office environment? Do you enjoy a lot of physical exertion or prefer sitting calmly while you work? Do you need to express your creativity, or do you enjoy analysis and research? Do you feel the need to travel or prefer to stay near home? What are you drawn to in your free time? What interests occupy your mind when you're alone in the car or taking a walk? As you're answering these questions, it may help to start with specifics—for example, you like hiking, playing in the yard with your kids, trying new recipes, compiling reports, reading histories or biographies, projecting stock trends, etc.—and then drawing some conclusions from those details. For example, if most of your preferred activities involve interacting with people, you can assume that you're highly relational and passionate about helping others. Or if most of your activities involve some degree of creativity, you probably are passionate about expressing yourself and may be called to communicate truth and impact hearts in unconventional ways. Even your hobbies—things you'll never get paid for—can tell you a lot about the things you're drawn to. You can begin to notice trends about your preferences and come to some conclusions about the desires of your heart.

## YOUR PATH TO FULFILLMENT

As you go through this exercise, try to put aside any assumptions you've already made about your calling. Write down any passions and interests that come to mind, even if you don't think they relate to your mission in life. Try to dig down to discover what really stirs your heart—the things that get you really motivated and excited about life. You may not be able to discern how those things relate to your overall calling yet, but you can begin to discern what they tell you about yourself. The bottom line is that God has put certain passions within you; deep in your core, and those passions will inevitably fuel the specific purpose He created you for. Linking the passions with the purpose may be a process, but it's an exciting one. While many people assume that God's will for their life will probably be difficult, boring, or unsatisfying, you can pursue His will with the joy of knowing that there's a connection between His purpose and your deepest desires. His calling isn't an unwelcome obligation; it's the path to your fulfillment.

> The bottom line is that God has put certain passions within you; deep in your core, and those passions will inevitably fuel the specific purpose He created you for.

Now that you've taken a long look at your passions, let's explore the other point at the bottom of the triangle: your talents and skills. God's purpose is usually evident in His design. A greyhound's small, lightweight body was made to run fast, for example; a dachshund's wasn't. An eagle's wings were created to enable him to soar high above the earth; a chicken was clearly made for an entirely different purpose. So what are you good at? What do people rely on you to be able to do? Do friends always seem to seek your advice? Are you physically strong and athletic? Are you detail-oriented and analytical? Are you a deep thinker focused on life's biggest questions? Are you an articulate speaker? Can you make an audience laugh? Or are you a more effective communicator in one-on-one conversations? Are you a gifted writer or an inspired artist? Or are you good with facts and statistics? There's no limit to the questions you could ask to reveal your capabilities and aptitudes, and you may already have a pretty good idea of what you do well. But also consider your potential—the natural talent you have that hasn't been developed yet, or the spiritual gifts you've seen glimpses of but haven't yet fully cultivated. All of these qualify as your set of skills and gifts that God has given you and is refining in you.

> **You'll usually be able to recognize your gifts and skills as abilities that are difficult for others but come easily to you.**

You'll usually be able to recognize your gifts and skills as abilities that are difficult for others but come easily to you. When you're functioning in your gifts, you feel like the wind is at your back. It doesn't mean you never have any obstacles or challenges, but there's a flow to your life that feels like you're moving in the right direction. You fit with your design.

With the bottom corners of the Life Impact triangle completed, now it's time to look at the top, where God's purposes are accomplished. Let's go back to our definition of success: completing with excellence the mission that God has called us to accomplish. If each of us represents a "divine design" made up of what we do well (skills and gifts) and our unique passions (what we love to do), these two areas of our life intersect at a point that

> **Our particular mission fits with His overall plan in the world. That's our calling.**

fulfills God's purposes for us. Our particular mission fits with His overall plan in the world. That's our calling.

Living in light of your calling is what God intended for you all along. This is why you are who you are. Many people go through life pursuing success and find out at the end that their definition of success was wrong. They spend years climbing the ladder of success only to find that it's leaning against the wrong wall. But discovering God's purpose for your life and pursuing it, using your gifts and skills in a way that fits your passions, doesn't end in disappointment. This is the key to the fulfillment we're all looking for.

Some people aren't convinced of that. Many approach God's calling as part of a meaningful life but not all of it. Maybe they see their key to fulfillment as a perfect marriage that meets all their relational needs, or a hefty bank account that allows them to seek after-hours fulfillment on weekends and vacations. But God's purpose for our lives is comprehensive and brings meaning and passion to every aspect of our existence. It's possible to have a difficult marriage or hardly any money and still be fulfilled—*if* you know your purpose. The fact is that God is our ultimate relationship and our all-sufficient provider, and we can handle anything in life if we know we are accomplishing what we were put here to do. When we live according to our purpose, we have direction to guide our decisions, we won't be thrown off course by changing circumstances or bad days, we are filled with a sense of significance, we make the most of our time, and we have all the provision we need for our assignment. All of the obstacles that seem to stand in our way eventually have to bow to the mission God has given us. We have the ability and resolve to endure and persevere. As Paul urged in 1 Corinthians 9:24, we run the race with an eye on the prize.

If that's the case, our job is to realize our purpose, understand it, focus on it, and complete our mission with excellence. Finding our fulfillment in our relationship with God and the mission He has given us brings us into harmony with Him. This majestic, holy, all-powerful Creator of the universe designed us not for our own pleasure—or our own idea of success—but for His. And in doing so, He aligned our skills, talents, passions, and emotions in such a way that our souls will explode in immense joy as we know Him and submit to His plan for our lives. This is "the Fulfillment Factor"—doing what we were created to do for God.

> **He aligned our skills, talents, passions, and emotions in such a way that our souls will explode in immense joy as we know Him and submit to His plan for our lives.**

**BLUEPRINT FOR • LIFE**

*Chapter Four*

# To Infinity and Beyond

"I value all things only by the price they shall gain in eternity."

*~ John Wesley*

Union soldiers had burned Atlanta and overrun Tara, and Scarlett O'Hara was frantic about her future. Her father wasn't; he had slipped into a mild dementia to cope with the devastation of the South. But Scarlett, trying to reestablish some sense of a normal life on the old plantation, was running out of options. There were no food stores or crops, nothing of value to exchange for supplies, no means of support. The only currency in the family was a stack of Confederate bonds Mr. O'Hara had been saving for a rainy day.

"Oh, Pa . . . what are those papers?" Scarlett asked.

"Bonds," he replied. "They're all we've saved. All we have left. Bonds."

"But what kind of bonds, Pa?"

"Why, Confederate bonds of course, darling."

"Confederate bonds," Scarlett lamented. "What good are they to anybody?"

Indeed, what good is an investment in an economy that won't last? Scarlett's father had put all of his money into a currency that would soon become obsolete. He didn't know that at the time, of course; he was simply banking on the future he expected—a Confederate nation with its own growing economy. The problem was that he didn't see the future accurately. His lack of vision led to investments that would eventually become worthless.

We find ourselves with the same options. Do we invest in the future we can see with our own eyes? Do we work primarily to build bank accounts that will serve us in this world? Or does our vision need to be bigger than that? According to scripture, we are created to live forever. We have an eternal future. No Blueprint for Life makes any sense if we don't see "life" as everlasting. While many people invest in the spiritual equivalent of Confederate bonds, we have a golden opportunity to lay up treasure in heaven. The things we do today matter forever in eternity.

> **No Blueprint for Life makes any sense if we don't see "life" as everlasting.**

This creates a dilemma, doesn't it? On one hand, you want a fulfilling life on earth—a loving family, a passionate marriage, rich relationships with your kids, close friends, enjoyable hobbies, a fit body, healthy finances, and a successful career. On the other hand, you must also plan for eternity. And that means thinking beyond the next few decades to develop a Blueprint for Life that factors God's kingdom and your eternal rewards into the picture. After all, this earth is not our ultimate destination. And God's Word clearly explains that while everybody attains salvation the same way—we are saved by grace through faith, not on the basis of our works—heaven will not be the same for everybody once we get there. Your experience in eternity will be decided by the decisions you make and the things you do during your lifetime.

> **Your experience in eternity will be decided by the decisions you make and the things you do during your lifetime.**

Many Christians are startled by that truth. We are so used to emphasizing grace—the fact that our works can't earn us salvation—that we tend to dismiss the importance of works entirely. But scripture is clear. There is a judgment in which people enter eternal rest with God or eternal separation from Him, and that's determined entirely by whether or not they had faith in Jesus and His sacrifice for our sins. Our behavior can't earn this salvation for us. It's entirely by grace through faith. But there's also a judgment in which we receive rewards from God for the works we have done. We are told in 2 Corinthians 5:10 that we will all appear before the judgment seat of Christ and be rewarded according to what we have done. This has nothing to do with whether we receive eternal life but everything to do with our experience of it. What we do now makes a difference forever.

Jesus spoke of rewards often—He told parables about wise and unwise stewards and promised blessings in heaven for enduring persecution, making sacrifices, and serving others—and these rewards were always based on the decisions and actions of those who follow Him. How well did they invest their gifts and talents? How diligent were they about serving His purposes? These are the things that determine the rewards that we receive after we die. They don't determine our salvation, but they do impact the kind of experience we have in eternity. Heaven is a kingdom, not a communist state. Citizenship is free to all, but rewards will vary significantly from person to person.

This is why it's vital for your life blueprint to be designed from an eternal perspective. A lot of people are simply planning to get into heaven. Their detailed plans are for the next few decades, but their long-term plan is only about where they are going to spend eternity, not what life will be like when they get there. But Jesus was clear that we can maximize our kingdom contributions and our rewards in heaven. Everything we do during our lifetime has the potential to impact our experience in eternity.

When this concept of eternity really sinks in, it becomes one of the greatest motivating factors in our lives. We realize what an amazing opportunity we have to leverage our lives for incomprehensible rewards. It shapes virtually everything we do—how we use our time, how we spend our money, how we treat other people, and more. Every day becomes an exciting adventure, a treasure hunt for opportunities to make another eternal investment by touching someone else's life. We become even more motivated to create an intentional plan, a blueprint that not only takes us through our earthly lives but accounts for forever.

So when we think about our God-given talents and gifts, we need to ask ourselves how we can leverage them for God's glory. The same can be said of our assets and our time and our network of relationships. How can we use our here-and-now resources as an investment in

> **So when we think about our God-given talents and gifts, we need to ask ourselves how we can leverage them for God's glory.**

God's eternal kingdom? How can we be strategic about winning souls for heaven and making disciples who will bear eternal fruit and enjoy God's presence forever? How can we convert our earthly portfolio into a kingdom portfolio? How does the career we choose allow us to fulfill our God-given purpose—not just now but always?

> **Heaven will not be the same for everyone who goes there. How you spend your life is of monumental importance.**

## LIVE FOR THE LINE, NOT THE DOT

Eternity is a mind-boggling concept. It's hard to wrap our thoughts around it, but it's fun to try. Picture, for example, a dot about the size of a period on this page. The dot represents your life on earth. Now imagine a line starting at the dot and continuing across the room, out the door, and on through infinite outer space. The line represents your eternal life, going on forever. That little dot may not be very big—by comparison, it's hardly even visible—but that little moment of time determines how the rest of your eternal existence will be spent. So what you do in that moment of time is of monumental importance. When you design a blueprint for your life, it's absolutely essential to live for the entire line, not just for the dot.

Most people, even most Christians, plan their lives with an almost exclusive focus on the dot. Before we come to Christ, that's all we know to live for. Setting goals seems to be merely a matter of reconciling our wildest dreams with what's actually possible. We try to resolve that tension between what we wish we could have and what's realistic. For someone without an eternal focus, everything is inside the dot.

But Christians need to have a completely different mindset. The reality is that eternal life began for all of us, whether Christian or not, at our conception. We all live forever either in fellowship with God in an unfathomable, glorious paradise or in dark separation from God. When we come to Christ and receive the eternal life He offers, we have to start thinking about how the dot impacts the line. The tension we encounter is not between what we wish for and what's realistic; it's between our hope for this life and our hope for eternity. And as Jesus repeatedly taught, we can't serve two masters. We can't serve both the line and the dot. We can experience great blessings in both places, but we can't fall into the trap of trying to serve both interests. If we're not careful, our life in this age can be in direct conflict with our life in

> **We all live forever either in fellowship with God in an unfathomable, glorious paradise or in dark separation from God.**

eternity. And once we're there, we can't go back and make course corrections. We have to choose now which focus to have.

The Christian's life blueprint is founded on the idea that we are completely sold out to God as master. When you abandon all self-centered reasons for living and begin to pursue God's purpose for your life, the tension between the two agendas is automatically reconciled. In that moment, you acquire both provision for this life (Matthew 6:33) and treasure for the life to come (Matthew 6:20). As a Christian, you are not doomed to follow the ever-shifting pull of material things you want at the time. You have the secure path of God's purpose for your life—a plan that allows God to direct you toward His best. The evangelist D.L. Moody once commented that the greatest lesson he'd learned in life was to let God choose for him. He could dream of big things, but he didn't have to desperately pursue them. He was sold out to his Master, and his Master would provide everything he needed and more.

So as long as you keep the pursuit of your purpose in mind, you are free to dream big for your life. But what kind of dreams? If heaven is not the same for everyone who goes there, suddenly some of the things we've been dreaming about start to lose their luster.

## That Changes Everything

A funny thing happens in light of eternity. Suddenly, the value of everything changes. What was once of little value becomes priceless. And what was once valuable becomes worthless. Remember how we talked about God's value system being so radically different from ours? From a perspective that includes eternity, we can see why. Things that were immensely important within the dot aren't really important when you also look at the line. And many things that are significant in the line are hardly noticeable from a point of view within the dot. The treasures of God's kingdom are the only ones that last, and those with a view toward eternity will pursue them passionately.

We don't begin life with that perspective, but time has a way of correcting our nearsightedness. When we've lived long enough to get glimpses of the passing chapters of human history, we begin to see how transient life in this world can be. The landscape of history is scattered with poignant dramas that demonstrate the relentless march of time. Each one demonstrates how fleeting our lives can be. As we watch them roll by, human beings become smaller and smaller while God grows ever larger.

The story of Colonel Kazimierz Mastalerz dramatically illustrates how quickly time can leave our best efforts in its wake. Mastalerz was one of the most prestigious military men in Europe, a decorated soldier and one of the highest ranking leaders in Poland's Pomeranian Cavalry Brigade. Poland's military had reigned supreme in the 1920s and '30s, turning back numerous assaults and defending its borders tenaciously. Their training and horsemanship were unsurpassed, and their tacticians were top of the line. They had an international reputation for having some of the fiercest battalions in the world. But on Sept. 1, 1939, Col. Mastalerz peered through trees of the Tuchola forest and knew that Poland's string of victories was about to end.

A deep rumbling shook the ground, and the horses of the cavalry grew skittish. In the distance, trees cracked and fell to the ground. Through the mist, two motorized divisions of the Third Reich appeared. In the hours that followed, Polish soldiers on horseback fought a futile battle against German tanks and armored cars. People from two seemingly different worlds clashed as one passing era surrendered to the next generation. Mastalerz died by machine-gun fire from soldiers in tanks while commanding men on horses. Time and technology had advanced relentlessly, and everything changed.

The Polish army had legitimate goals. After World War I, the country had begun building a military sufficient to defend itself and had tested its progress in border skirmishes for two decades. The goal seemed to have been achieved. The problem was that Poland failed to plan far enough ahead. They had overlooked the realities of a new era. They had applied 1920s thinking to a 1940s world, and that oversight proved fatal.

## YOUR ETERNAL PORTFOLIO

If your life blueprint is to reflect an accurate perspective, you must factor in your ultimate destination in eternity. As the martyred missionary Jim Elliot once said, "He is no fool who gives up what

> "He is no fool who gives up what he cannot keep to gain what he cannot lose."
> -Jim Elliot

he cannot keep to gain what he cannot lose." The moment you leave this world, economy as you know it will change. Things that were once considered valuable in this world will suddenly become useless to you. And in an instant, many of the things that this world often overlooks will become valuable. Make sure your blueprint factors this in.

To pursue a goal, you must first define the goal. Likewise, to pursue a Blueprint for Life, you must first decide on a definition of life. If you define life as the 70-80 year period that follows birth, you will create a blueprint that applies to that time frame. But if you embrace the idea that eternal life never ends, it will make you think long and hard about what you deem valuable. That 401k might buy thousands of rounds of golf during your retirement years, but then what? And those promotions at work might give you a sense of accomplishment throughout your career, but what will they be worth in a few hundred years? Are you truly ready to embrace a long-term perspective? Are you ready to create a blueprint for *eternal* life?

> **Are you truly ready to embrace a long-term perspective? Are you ready to create a blueprint for eternal life?**

Everyone has an eternal portfolio. It contains the items of eternal value that you have accumulated so far. When you are a good steward of your time and earthly resources, your life contributes to God's kingdom and your portfolio grows.

So as you plan ahead, it's important to consider what things will truly hold their value in the centuries to come. What things that seem valuable today will become worthless? And what seemingly worthless things might become priceless? You will need to know these things in order to draw up a blueprint that will hold its value. Hundreds of stories and lessons in the Bible explain which things have eternal worth and which ones don't. The greatest commandment is to love God with everything in us, so clearly that has eternal significance. It's why we were made. That includes worshiping Him and reflecting His glory. But in terms of what we do—the work and activities we engage in that honor Him and His purposes—virtually all of the Bible's instructions seem to revolve directly or indirectly around the concept of loving and serving each other for the purpose of making disciples. Jesus said it this way:

> *"Therefore go and make disciples of all nations, baptizing them in the name of the Father and of the Son and of the Holy Spirit, and teaching them to obey everything I have commanded you. And surely I am with you always, to the very end of the age."*
>
> **Matthew 28:19-20 NIV**

Those were the final instructions He gave His followers before He left earth. Notice He didn't mention anything about attending church each week, organizing social events, or volunteering to be a youth group adviser. He didn't remind them of the Ten Commandments one more time. He was announcing a singular mission: make disciples. Sure, attending church may be a part of it. Social events may be your area of service. And you may be involved in the youth group along the way. All of these activities may serve the overall purpose of making disciples. But you'll need to make sure that's the bottom line. If your efforts are not contributing directly to the overall mission—if your motives are to make a name for yourself, expand your network, or just to keep yourself occupied—then they might not add anything to your eternal portfolio. It's not enough just to keep a religious checklist that you update from time to time. God isn't very impressed with religious activity. He's purely relational, and virtually every aspect of His mission is relational. Our role is to know and love Him and then to help others know and love Him. Regardless of our career and activities, our purpose needs to somehow reflect this mission.

Here's how Jesus explained it:

> *"Not all who sound religious are really godly people. They may refer to me as 'Lord,' but still won't get to heaven. For the decisive question is whether they obey my Father in heaven. At the Judgment many will tell me, 'Lord, Lord, we told others about you and used your name to cast out demons and to do many other great miracles.' But I will reply, 'You have never been mine. Go away, for your deeds are evil.'"*
>
> **Matthew 7:21-23 TLB**

So this is what we need to ask ourselves: What can I do that would contribute to the fulfillment of Jesus' instructions? In what ways can I influence people to become a part of or to grow in God's kingdom? Don't think in terms of traditional ministry roles unless that happens to be what God has called you to do. The church has focused too long only on activity within the church and in specialized professions that reach beyond its walls. Think of yourself instead as a kingdom citizen who is called to infiltrate society with the good news of Jesus. How can you represent the nature of God where you live and work? How can you demonstrate the culture of God's kingdom in a way that impacts those around you? How can you reflect His glory in your character? your words? your actions? How can you convey the themes of His truth in your creative expression? How can you pray for those around you? How can you support the work of the local church in carrying out its mission? How can you support those who take the message overseas or into hard-to-reach communities? The answers to these questions will inevitably involve your spiritual life, your finances, your relationships, your career, your community activities—everything. Think outside the box. Your blueprint may look very traditional, or it may appear radical or surprising or completely unconventional. The point is that it somehow needs to reflect the overall mission. If you want to be rich in a currency that's going to hold its value, this is how you do it.

Making disciples ultimately means introducing Jesus to those who don't know Him and providing encouragement to those who do know Him. In both cases, we leverage our resources to create environments of loving and serving in order to share God's truth with others. This doesn't mean you must be an evangelist or a preacher. It simply means you use whatever resources God has given you to contribute to the mission. There are many ways you can steward your resources to be involved in the process. You become an ambassador of God's kingdom—even a vessel of His own Spirit—wherever you go.

## TAKING INVENTORY

So how much of this currency have you accumulated in life so far? Is it random pocket change—like the coins you find in your suitcase after a trip out of the country? Is there enough to buy something substantial with what you've amassed? Or maybe you've been socking it away so long that the interest is compounding faster than you can count it. Take an inventory of your portfolio. How much of it is invested in things that are primarily of earthly value? How much in things primarily of eternal value? Yes, many of your investments will apply to both of these categories. The love and support you give your family, for example, certainly takes care of their temporal needs while also strengthening your relationships with them and influencing them with kingdom values. But where is your primary focus? Which area is your portfolio designed to serve? You'll want to have a healthy portfolio that reflects faithful service and that will reap everlasting rewards.

By the end of Schindler's List, Oskar Schindler has already saved countless Jewish lives from German concentration camps. But instead of being satisfied with the opportunities he has successful taken advantage of, he is struck by the opportunities he has missed. Filled with passion for his unfinished business, he begins to itemize that untapped potential. If only he had sold his car, he could have saved more lives by bribing more German officials. And if he had sold his Nazi Party badge, he could have rescued at least one more person. "I could have done more," he laments again and again. That's probably very similar to the feeling many of us might have when we get to heaven and see the opportunities we missed to invest in the lives of others. How many more disciples could we have encouraged? How many more people could we have introduced to God? How many more dark corners of this world could we have brightened with God's light? This won't be a cry of despair; we'll still be celebrating all of God's extravagant rewards for the things we did. What if we could go ahead and live with that perspective now? What if we develop a blueprint that incorporates that approach? We would maximize our potential both now and in the age to come.

> **When we use our time, our money, our influence, or other collateral to serve the physical and spiritual needs of others and build relationships founded in God's love, we exchange this world's currency for eternal currency.**

When we use our time, our money, our influence, or other collateral to serve the physical and spiritual needs of others and build relationships founded in God's love, we exchange this world's currency for eternal currency. Paul wrote, "I've become just about every sort of servant there is in my attempts to lead those I meet into a God-saved life" (1 Corinthians 9:22 MSG). Think of the compound interest on an internal investment! The dividends never end. No one ever regrets leveraging temporal currency for eternal returns. It's the best investment we could ever make.

Everybody has unique interests, resources, and skills. You may also be uniquely positioned, because of your circumstances or status, to perform certain duties or contribute certain assets. Your job throughout the rest of this book—as you think through your career, finances, relationships, and physical qualities—is to identify ways you can directly support this mission with your whole life. God had something special in mind when he gave you your allotment of time, talent, and treasure. And now you have the opportunity to plan your life in a way that will reflect enormous value in the coming economy.

> **And now you have the opportunity to plan your life in a way that will reflect enormous value in the coming economy.**

*Chapter Five*

# What You Focus on Expands

"As a man thinketh so is he."

*~ Proverbs 23:7*

It was supposed to be impossible. That was they said—human beings can't run a mile in less than four minutes. For years, the world's fastest athletes had stepped onto a track with this barrier in mind, and every single time their expectations were confirmed. The theory that no one could run a four-minute mile had been proven again and again.

But on May 6, 1954, Roger Bannister faced some of the world's fastest men at Oxford's Iffley Road track near London and ran the fastest mile ever recorded—just under four minutes. The news of this feat shocked the world, but what happened next was even more amazing. Less than two months later, Australia's John Landy broke Bannister's record with another sub-four-minute mile. New Zealand's Peter Snell did even better later that year. In the months that followed, dozens more runners broke the four-minute barrier. This "impossible" feat soon became commonplace.

For centuries, four minutes had stood as a limit of human achievement. Every man who had stepped onto a track had bowed submissively to this common preconception. But when Bannister shattered the myth and proved that a four-minute mile was possible, he essentially issued an invitation for runners everywhere to join him. He hadn't introduced a new running technique or a special way to train. There was nothing unusual about his approach. He simply changed their notion of what was possible. He contributed the one thing that had been missing for all those years: belief. Once other runners saw it done, they had no choice but to believe it could be done. If Bannister could do it, so could they. The rest is history.

## Train Your Brain

Bannister's contemporaries were limited by one thing: their level of belief. They wanted to break the four-minute mile, and were physically capable of it. Always had been. But only when they believed it could be done did they succeed. Belief was the missing ingredient. Henry Ford said, "Whether you think you can or can't do something, you are absolutely right." He understood the power of our minds and our hearts to shape our lives and the world around us. The expectations you have will inevitably impact the experiences you have. Your level of belief is often the only thing that holds you where you are.

> **Your level of belief is often the only thing that holds you where you are.**

That may seem like nothing more than the power of positive thinking, but it's really a solid spiritual truth. The Bible has much to say about vision, dreams, faith, hope, works, and achieving goals. These concepts have often been used by other belief systems in a way that makes Christians want to shy away from them—the misuses and abuses are numerous—so many Christian teachers today scarcely mention them for fear of being misunderstood. But these concepts weren't invented by mystic new-age teachers or by preachers of the prosperity gospel. They shouldn't be controversial at all if we understand them biblically. The Bible contains some of the most authoritative instruction on how the brain works and how we can leverage the power of our minds to accomplish things we never thought possible.

A central goal of Blueprint for Life is to empower a new generation of Christians not only with a vision of God's purpose for their lives, but also with an understanding of how a mind that is transformed, sober, and devoted to God's purposes is able to move mountains. When you truly understand what it means to "take every thought captive," you will discover a new level of lucidity about your life and your goals for fulfilling your purpose. Sigmund Freud pointed out that "the mind is like an iceberg; it floats with one-seventh of its bulk above water." When your mind truly implements biblical truth, things change.

People who study the human brain tell us that we understand vastly more about how our minds work than we used to—but we still know very little. The brain is still one of the greatest mysteries of God's creation. Your mind can accomplish things you've never thought possible, and if you learn to take your thoughts captive, you can live with purpose in every area of life. With focus, you can retrain your brain to think in different and better ways that support how your life was intended to be. Frank Outlaw described the renewing of our minds this way:

*Watch your thoughts, for they become your words.*

*Watch your words, for they become your actions.*

*Watch your actions, for they become your habits.*

*Watch your habits, for they become your character.*

*Watch your character, for it becomes your destiny.*

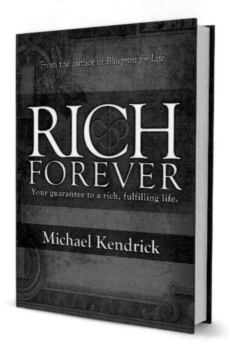

# If you've always dreamed of becoming rich, *forever is the time to do it.*

Join author Michael Kendrick on his journey of making tens of millions of dollars, losing them, then making even more again. You will learn life changing principles that will help you succeed and possibly even become wealthy in the process. More importantly, you will learn how to amass the kind of wealth that lasts *forever*.

For more information or to purchase, please visit richforever.com.

All of us have struggled at times with negative thoughts, either from learned patterns in our past relationships or from distorted perspectives we've been tempted to pick up along the way. And you've probably noticed that you can't really change your behavior without changing the thoughts behind your behavior. So scripture urges us to change our thinking, to renew our minds, to reject our own faulty perspectives and embrace God's. This process involves focusing on Him, directing our hearts toward worship, praise, and gratitude, studying and believing the truth He has revealed, and many other approaches. We are called to be sober-minded—that is, to exercise self-discipline in our thought life; to have transformed minds that shape our character and reflect the nature of God; and to have devoted minds that have deep affection for Him and are completely dedicated to His ways. When this is our state of mind, many of the limits we thought constrained us disappear. We are equipped to live with faith and focus. And our faith is the kind that can break barriers and move mountains.

## THE MISSING LINK

If your experience in life is often determined by what you believe, one of your first objectives in creating your life blueprint is to lift the lid on your level of belief. You don't want your own unbelief to be your first limitation. This is an important truth. Your own level of belief is likely to be the biggest limitation in terms of discovering all that God has in store for you. People tend to think smaller for themselves than God does. As a result, God may want to do more

> **Your own level of belief is likely to be the biggest limitation in terms of discovering all that God has in store for you.**

with your lives than you realize or imagine. If you set your sights on something less, you could miss Him.

This is a clear pattern between God and His people. When God told Sarah, Abraham's wife, about the nation that would come from her womb, she laughed with disbelief. When Moses heard that he was to convince Pharaoh to let God's people go, he said he was inadequate for the task. God overcame these limitations in their own minds, but it was a process. He had to convince them and give them time to believe what He had said. Today they are mentioned in the New Testament as people of great faith, but they didn't necessarily start out that way. They had to align their minds with what He said about their lives. So do we.

> **If God revealed to you the full scope of what He would like to do in your life, how would you react?**

If God revealed to you the full scope of what He would like to do in your life, how would you react? If it's a big dream, the natural tendency for most of us would be to pass if off as a fantasy or the lingering effects of last night's indigestion. We grow to expect such ordinary things from God that we don't leave much room for big dreams. Sometimes it seems that the average person wouldn't even recognize God's will unless it's disguised as something mundane.

What you believe about yourself determines your potential. If you don't believe your life is capable of holding a big vision, you'll never embrace it and pursue it. Without belief, your brain will shut down any serious effort to make something happen. When a circus elephant spends the first years of its life chained to a stake, it only takes a small rope to hold him there even when he's fully grown. The mere suggestion that he is restrained is enough to make him stay put.

The same can be true for you. If God gives you a big vision—a dream of lifetime proportions—it can be an overwhelming thing. Your tendency will be to stay in your comfort zone.

## Baby Steps

If our beliefs determine our potential, we need to answer a really pressing question: How can we get the right beliefs? The key to acquiring confident belief is in recognizing your purpose follows a process. It's always a progression. You don't have to get from where you are now to the fulfillment of a huge vision in one giant leap. That can be overwhelming. But when you break a vision down into smaller steps, you can develop the confidence necessary to keep your heart in the vision. Rather than allowing yourself to become paralyzed by the enormity of your goal, you can develop confidence by focusing only on the next step—the one within your reach.

King David was a great example of this process when he was a young man. On the surface, his confident decision to face the giant warrior Goliath may have seemed like a naïve, uninformed burst of outrage. But he wasn't acting rashly. He wasn't trying to impress the teenage girls or vastly underestimating his opponent's size. His confidence was the result of a faith that had begun long before he met Goliath, and it had been growing over time.

Early on in life, David had somehow gotten a vision—a strong conviction that God would protect him from any enemies he faced. Perhaps he embraced the idea immediately, or maybe he needed convincing. We don't know for sure. But by the time he faced Goliath, we know he had tested the hypothesis several times. When Saul confronted David with his shortcomings as a warrior, David explained his vision and his faith to the king. Their conversation went like this:

> *"'Don't be ridiculous!' Saul replied. 'How can a kid like you fight with a man like him? You are only a boy, and he has been in the army since he was a boy!' But David persisted. 'When I am taking care of my father's sheep,' he said, 'and a lion or a bear comes and grabs a lamb from the flock, I go after it with a club and take the lamb from its mouth. If it turns on me, I catch it by the jaw and club it to death. I have done this to both lions and bears, and I'll do it to this heathen Philistine too, for he has defied the armies of the living God! The Lord who saved me from the claws and teeth of the lion and the bear will save me from this Philistine!' Saul finally consented, 'All right, go ahead,' he said, 'and may the Lord be with you!'"*

> **1 Samuel 17:33-37 TLB**

Do you see the progression in David's account? He tried it out on lions. He perfected it against bears. Now he's ready for the next challenge: a very big warrior named Goliath. That's the picture of a growing faith. It's also our model for cultivating belief in our God-given goals.

## CULTIVATING BELIEF

> **Belief dies without vision, and vision dies without belief.**

Belief dies without vision, and vision dies without belief. The key is to keep your goals in sight. One way to do that is to set goals that don't overstretch your belief. We tend to be nearsighted believers; we can only believe when the goal is close enough to reality. Our capacity to believe expands with experience and time—some people have the audacity to dream big and trust God to get them there one day—but most of us have to start with something smaller. So before you go after a goal, check yourself. Can you really see it? Or is it a bit fuzzy? If you don't feel like you can almost reach out and touch it, then you probably need an easier goal first. Don't abandon the long-term goal, but put it on the shelf for a while and pick out an easier one that leads toward it. As God enables you to accomplish your interim goals, it will provide affirmation that you are on the way to accomplishing His will for your life.

Creating a Blueprint for Life is not just a matter of figuring out where you need to go. It's also deciding how to get there. The most important skill in this process is your ability to break the trip down into reasonable segments. These segments need to be small enough to preserve and grow your confidence, but they also need to be large enough to stretch your faith and actually move you toward the goal.

> **Creating a Blueprint for Life is not just a matter of figuring out where you need to go. It's also deciding how to get there.**

The problem with many New Year's resolutions is that they don't strike this balance. They focus on a long-term goal, but there's very little connection to the present. So it's only a matter of time before the original vision gets clouded by the clutter of living. After six weeks of hard dieting and no sign of the end result on the horizon, you start to ask yourself, "Now, why was it I decided to torture myself like this?" The goal is a good one, but the steps to get there are too far apart or too intimidating to conquer. Somewhere along the way, belief dies.

The strategy of blueprinting your life involves creating short-range goals that will enable you to keep your vision closely linked to the present. Seeing is believing. When you can clearly see the goal well enough to almost reach out and touch it, then it's easy to believe. Your confidence is bolstered and your vision thrives. That's what Roger Bannister did for his colleagues, and that's what a blueprint will do for you. Your Blueprint for Life develops stepping-stones that form a path to your ultimate destination. As each milestone is reached, your confidence grows, your vision crystallizes, and your motivation skyrockets.

Belief is not a magic wand, of course. You can't just "believe" God into doing something that's not part of His plan. This isn't about having faith in the power of faith. It's having faith in God. More belief will not suddenly make things work out like you wanted. God made us with certain limits. But those limits usually aren't as confining as the ones we place on ourselves through our small vision and lack of belief. So when you set your goals, be certain that they aren't hindered by fear or shortsightedness, and also that they aren't tainted by greed and self-centeredness. Remember, you're looking for God's purposes for your life, not your own. Know where you're going, trust God to get you there, and keep your eyes focused on the vision. Belief won't make it happen magically, but it will open the way for it to happen in God's power.

## THE POWER OF FOCUS

> There's a second component for pursuing your goals that's just as crucial: FOCUS.

Belief is the first component you'll need to pursue any goal. You have to believe it can happen and then follow the baby steps to get there. But there's a second component for pursuing your goals that's just as crucial: FOCUS. Your life blueprint is like an architect's plans. It contains numerous views and details to show how the plans will become reality. But many people get distracted from, drawn away from, or hindered from sticking with the plans. And without implementing specific plans, knowing your purpose has limited value. The principle of focus will help you execute the plans God gives you.

Your ability to follow through on your goals in life corresponds directly with your ability to keep them in focus. Your direction in life is determined by whatever is front-and-center in your mind at any given moment. If you become distracted from your main objective, your goals will drift idly to the deep recesses of your brain where they will eventually fade away. But if you apply a few techniques to take your thoughts captive, you can live with purpose in every stride of life.

Grasping this principle is like grasping the steering wheel of your life. You can use it to point yourself in virtually any direction you choose. In a typical day, there are thousands of things that compete for our attention, yet you can only give your attention to one idea at a time. Your goals must overcome the clutter of daily distractions if you are to stand a chance of following through. Long-term, con-

> **Grasping this principle is like grasping the steering wheel of your life. You can use it to point yourself in virtually any direction you choose.**

sistent attention to a predetermined goal will require you to take an intentional approach to life. You can't leave it to chance.

Your life blueprint includes mechanisms for bringing you back to your main priorities on a regular basis. By following a blueprint for your life, your daily life is tied to your goals. And your goals are tied to your purpose. In other words, your blueprint is a focus mechanism that will keep your

> **By following a blueprint for your life, your daily life is tied to your goals. And your goals are tied to your purpose.**

attention on your ultimate purpose and connect it with your daily activities. It's a bridge between point A and point B in your life.

Here's how focus works: All learning is based on repetition and associations. Our brains prioritize data based on patterns of repetition. Every time an idea is repeated, we increase the number of associations that correspond with that idea. The more we are exposed to an idea, the more likely we are to recall it in everyday situations.

Advertisers understand this dynamic completely. They rely on it to sell their products. They show us images of smiling people eating their food, driving their cars, or cleaning the house with their soap. And, most importantly, they repeat their product name. They spend millions of dollars to gain access to our heads for just a few seconds. They are banking on the fact that they can create associations in our brains that will prompt us to recall their name in everyday situations and buy their products.

The more associations you develop with a concept or idea, the more central it becomes to your thinking. Your life today is a complex network of the associations that have been created during your lifetime. Now just imagine if you could influence those associations—or create new ones—to establish connections that lead you naturally and effortlessly toward your life goals. Once you understand what goes on in your brain during this process, it's really simple to do.

Suppose you're stuck in traffic, for example, surrounded by hundreds of cars of various makes and models as you creep along the interstate. As you patiently move along, you hardly pay attention to the other vehicles and motorists around you. But suddenly, out of the clutter, your eye is drawn to one car in particular . . . a couple of lanes over . . . and partly obscured by a tractor-trailer rig up ahead. You can barely see it, but it jumps out at you like it was the only other car on the highway. It's a red Jeep . . . just like the one you've been thinking about buying!

Relatively speaking, there's nothing that attention-grabbing about the Jeep. But you've been gazing at those cars for weeks, telling your brain it's more important than the others. You've created numerous associations. As a result, all it took was one little glimpse of the Jeep's back bumper to catch your attention.

## INTENTIONAL FOCUS

You can see how this principle already works passively in your life, without any effort on your part. Now imagine using it proactively to steer your attention toward the ideas that are most important in your life—your goals! If you will repeat those ideas intentionally, at specified intervals, they will soon rise to the forefront of your mind.

As we've discussed, the Bible calls this process "renewing your mind." Our thoughts precede our actions. Therefore, our lives tend to form around the things that are most prominent in our minds. As Alexander Graham Bell said, "Con-centrate all your thoughts on the task at hand. The sun's rays do not burn until brought to a focus." When you apply this same principle to your

> **Our lives tend to form around the things that are most prominent in our minds.**

goals, your mind will begin to prioritize your actions around the things that support your objectives.

That's why it's so important to have a plan and to focus on it. God hasn't called us to wander aimlessly, unaware of where we're headed. Obviously, we need to be flexible enough for Him to change our direction at any moment. But we aren't spiritual tumbleweeds that drift wherever the wind blows, oblivious to its movements. We cooperate with the Holy Spirit in our lives to walk in the direction He's calling us. That means having a kingdom perspective and being very intentional about the ways that perspective shapes our decisions. We are people of purpose who carry eternal values in our hearts.

## INVESTMENTS OF THE MIND

> **Jesus said that our hearts would be wherever our treasure is (Matthew 6:21).**

Jesus said that our hearts would be wherever our treasure is (Matthew 6:21). That seems to suggest that our focus compounds exponentially when we are intentional. He used the word "treasure" to refer to the things we consider valuable, whatever they happen to be. Whatever we tend to value, that's where our heart tends to grow. Our focus expands around the things we prioritize, whether it's our time, our money, ourselves—whatever. Conventional wisdom would say that whatever is important to us is where we'll spend our time, but Jesus turns that around to show that it works the other way too. Whatever we spend our time on becomes more and more important to us. That gives us the power to develop our interests around the things that will benefit us the most. We aren't victims of whatever seems to come naturally. We can be intentional about what we value and the treasures we cultivate in our lives.

Jesus went on to say,

> *"The lamp of the body is the eye. If therefore your eye is good, your whole body will be full of light. But if your eye is bad, your whole body will be full of darkness."*

> Matthew 6:22-23

Though the immediate context of this passage is about finances and generosity, Jesus is tapping into the larger principle of focus. It's as if He's saying, "As the eye goes, so goes the rest of you." Whatever you look at, listen to, and think about—those things determine where you will end up. If you feast your eyes on good, your whole body will tend to walk in the light. If you pore over Jeep brochures, your whole body will be highly attuned to those vehicles. As Jesus points out, you can fill yourself with good things, or you can fill yourself with bad things; it's completely up to you. Whatever you repeat, that's what your mind will prioritize.

## AN EMPTY SLATE

So here's the question: What do you want your life to accomplish? You can probably identify several dreams immediately, but have you ever really thought about that question thoroughly? Take some time to try an exercise in dreaming. Grab a piece of paper and a pen and list as many things you dream of doing in your lifetime. Don't think

> **So here's the question: What do you want your life to accomplish?**

> **If you knew you couldn't fail, what would you want to do in your life?**

about money; it's not an issue. Neither is experience or whether you think your dreams are realistic or not. Reach for the stars. If you knew you couldn't fail, what would you want to do in your life? List places you want to visit, people you want to meet, accomplishments you want to achieve, possessions you want to own, scenarios you want to live out, and so on. Don't limit yourself to a few—make it a long list. What positions would you like to hold? What awards do you want to win? Who would you most want to have dinner with? Where would you buy a vacation home? What kind of spiritual influence do you want to have? What sports would you play? What countries do you want to visit? What languages would you be able to speak? What instruments would you be able to play? Spend about 15 minutes dreaming without restraint.

After you've finished the dreaming part of the exercise, fast-forward to your last years. Imagine sitting on a porch swing looking back over your life. With your previous list in mind, begin listing all the things you want to make sure you've done—the things that, if left undone, would cause you to look back with deep regret. Your previous list was about reaching for the stars; this one focuses on the down-to-earth aspects of your life. Since you're looking back, go ahead and put your statements in the past tense: "I've had a long and distinguished military career." "I put my children through college." "I've had the love and respect of my children and enjoyed the satisfaction of seeing them live with the character I instilled in them." "I saved enough money for retirement." "I made my spouse feel loved." And on and on. Like your reach-for-the-stars list, this one should cover multiple areas of your life—relationships, career, physical health, finances, spiritual growth, etc. Stick to the non-negotiables—the things you simply must have in order not to be disappointed when you've lived out your years.

Once you've completed this list, choose one major objective to focus on right now and determine at least five steppingstones that would lead you toward the fulfillment of that goal. At times you will want to come back to this list and do the same for other major objectives. As you develop steps toward your goals, you may find yourself streamlining your life in order to serve those goals. You may need to put some activities and directions aside or pick up some new ones that will help you accomplish your purposes. This exercise will help you begin to bring your life into greater focus.

Whatever your blueprint calls for, it's within your power to begin focusing intentionally on the things that support it. Instead of standing by passively while your interests gravitate naturally to whatever comes along, you can be proactive and make sure you not only have fun but also make progress.

Your goals are ideas to be reinforced. As you intentionally focus on the steppingstones that lead you toward your long-term plans, your brain will begin to take notice. It only takes a little reinforcing. This book will walk you through five key areas of your life and prompt you to determine goals that are important to you. We'll take a look at several techniques to reinforce those ideas throughout the rest of your life. At the end of this process, you'll not only know where you're going, but you'll experience a new level of focus and confidence to make sure you get there.

# BLUEPRINT FOR· LIfE.

## Chapter Six

# The Big Five

"Blessed are the balanced; they shall outlast everyone."

*~ Rick Warren*

The business world is full of stories of people who climbed the corporate ladder and arrived at the top of their company—high-powered executives who, for one reason or another, now stand head and shoulders above everyone else climbing that same ladder. The political world has its stories too, as does the sports world, the entertainment world, and just about any other arena of culture you can think of. The highest achievers do whatever it takes to reach their goals. And as we begin to think of specific examples of these highly successful people we can probably notice a common theme in the lives of many of them: unbalanced lives.

> **Many people have stellar careers but extremely broken relationships because they have been overly focused on the one area they want to excel in.**

Think about it. In a competitive world, who rises to the top? Not only those who have skills and gifts and passions, but also those who put in the most time and effort—those who are willing to pay the high cost of "success" at the expense of other vital areas of their lives. Many people have stellar careers but extremely broken relationships because they have been overly focused on the one area they want to excel in. They have neglected the people who are most important to them in order to earn the admiration of those who aren't. Some have nearly killed themselves physically—with stress, high blood pressure, unbalanced diets, lack of exercise, etc.—in their quest to fill their lives with the achievements they desire. In recent years, we've seen politicians, football coaches, and entertainers "retire" just to get away from the consuming, obsessive lifestyle required to stay at the top of their field. Their finances and popularity usually aren't lacking, but they have finally understood that there's more to life than a healthy bank account and the esteem of fans and voters. They have finally had enough of 18-hour work days and have confessed that their families and their own health suffer from their pursuit of excellence. They have realized how important it is to have balance in every area of life.

## TRUE SUCCESS INCLUDES BALANCE

Just as an "eternal perspective" is very important to avoid a misguided and wasted life, so is balance. Without balance, we will not be able to go the distance and create a life that is pleasing to God. As you begin to consider a blueprint for your life, you'll need to make sure it covers your whole personhood—every area of your life. It needs to take into account your spiritual growth, your relationships, your physical well-being, your finances, and your career. Success in only one or two areas isn't success in God's value system. He designed us to be whole and well-rounded.

> Just as an "eternal perspective" is very important to avoid a misguided and wasted life, so is balance.

The word "balance" doesn't usually stir up feelings of excitement, but balance among five areas of life will help you create daily life strategies that:

1) Develop an intimate relationship with your heavenly Father

2) Ensure rich relationships with your spouse, children, parents, and peers

3) Maintain your physical and mental fitness to ensure energy and capacity to meet your life goals

4) Prioritize the four roles of your finances: tithes, provision, offerings, and abundance

5) Align your career with your overall Blueprint for Life, allowing your career to serve your goals of a rich fulfilling life of balance, which has significant impact to God's Kingdom

You've probably known people who are really good at something but who have allowed that part of their lives to take over and crowd out nearly everything else. The highly effective career executive who is admired at work has often spent late nights and long weekends at the office—at the expense of the spouse and kids. Those brilliant scholars whose research is changing their field have often conducted that research at the neglect of their own health or financial stability. The typical American family spends much of the week running ragged—trying to get their over-involved kids to every practice, eating fast-food meals on the fly in the minivan, over-emphasizing SAT scores and perfect grades long before college is even on the horizon, doing everything they can do to excel yet hardly having any time to be together and enjoy each other. Most of us know men who have immersed themselves in their job in order to earn more money and provide for the family—a large house with a pool, private school, nice cars, memorable vacations—yet are depriving the family of the one thing they need most: Dad at home. A father so consumed with his work, even when it's for the sake of the family, misses precious moments like laughing together at the dinner table or reading a bedtime story to the kids at night. It's easy to get caught up in a lifestyle that's intended to provide security and material blessings yet also undermines relationships and health. It's one of the pitfalls of our culture.

There's nothing wrong with providing well for your family or making sacrifices to be successful. Not at all. And there are many successful CEOs and scholars and creative people who haven't sacrificed their balance to arrive at their success. But when those efforts to provide or excel result in an unbalanced life, you'll miss the joy and meaning you're striving so diligently to acquire. If the demands of your career leave no time for your spiritual growth, is it worthwhile? If you achieve all your financial goals and ruin your health in

> **When those efforts to provide or excel result in an unbalanced life, you'll miss the joy and meaning you're striving so diligently to acquire.**

the process, have you gained anything? Even if your spiritual pursuits— ministry and mission—are impacting God's kingdom but your children wonder where you are, have you lost something? You can only live the life of impact you were designed for when you're following God's blueprint for every area of life.

You don't need to look far to see many examples of people whose lives are out of balance, whether it's the family who is overwhelmed by debt or the person who lacks the simple discipline of regular exercise and becomes overweight and unhealthy. Some people are so focused on the visible parts of their lives that they neglect their spiritual development, while others are so "spiritual" that their finances, relationships and health are in ruin. Their spiritual growth hasn't had any practical effects. Balance calls for us to give focused attention to several areas of our lives simultaneously, not allowing any to suffer from lack of attention or allowing any to become too big. Balance will create harmony and peace in our lives as we pursue our plan to live the life that God has called us to live. God is a God of order and balance—nature is a great example of that—and He will not call us to violate His principles or priorities to pursue anything that is not of Him. If we think He is leading us yet our choices aren't creating balance, something is missing. He speaks His wisdom and direction into every aspect of our existence.

## THE WHEEL OF FORTUNE

Think of the components of your life as spokes of a wheel. Each one works with the others to create an overall effect. When all of the spokes are tuned up, the wheel is nice and round, and the journey is smooth. If one or two of the spokes comes up short, the whole wheel will bounce and jump. Over time, an imbalance can cause the wheel to destroy itself.

> **The categories of your life are designed to work together. God did not create us as a collection of separate components, as though we could be compartmentalized; He created us as whole beings, fully integrated.**

The categories of your life are designed to work together. God did not create us as a collection of separate components, as though we could be compartmentalized; He created us as whole beings, fully integrated. Our spokes have to function together. The categories of our lives require a certain amount of balance between them. Neglect any one of them, and eventually you'll pay a price. Balance them properly, and the overall effort is advanced. In fact, not only do they need balance; they also need to work together. They impact each other more than we might think. Your physical condition can impact your spiritual attitudes, and vice versa. Your relationships can impact your finances, and vice versa. Your career will define many of your relationships and shape your spiritual growth, and your relationships and spiritual growth will affect your career. For better or worse, all these areas are tied together.

So when you build yourself up in one area but neglect another, you are undermining your own efforts. No amount of desire or good intentions will substitute for the expertise of each "person" inside you. Every part of you needs to show up and be "on the job." For example, no matter how committed you are to your family, your relationships with them will suffer if you never come home from the office. It's an unavoidable principle. You have to report for duty in each area.

So how rounded is your life? If the components of your life were spokes of a wheel, would they function together smoothly? Or are one or two spokes significantly shorter than the others? Are things rolling along smoothly? Or are you hopping and bouncing down the road of life? What does your life wheel look like?

In reality, balance doesn't have to mean that all the spokes are exactly the same length at each moment in time. You will have some areas that are more prominent than others at various periods in your life. For example, if you're a single mother, there might be seasons when you focus on certain areas for the long-term good. In addition, some areas require less time and energy than others. But all are very important. Over time, you should be growing in all of them. So as we go through the five aspects of your life in this book, it will be imperative to discover God's blueprint in each one and develop goals that help you become a balanced, well-rounded person.

## THE BIG FIVE

We've briefly mentioned the five areas that make up the Blueprint for Life model, but now let's introduce them in a little more depth.

**Spiritual**: Your spirit is the part of you that will live forever. It's what inhabits your physical body and gives it life. Your spirit determines your worldview and your perspective. It shapes your overall demeanor and your attitude. Your spirit is the conductor of a complex symphony of biochemical brain activity, locomotive and lingual expressions, and other physical cues that represent your being. Thoughts flow across the synapses of your brain, but the nature of your thoughts flows from your spirit.

> **Thoughts flow across the synapses of your brain, but the nature of your thoughts flows from your spirit.**

You can develop your spirit, simply maintain it, or neglect it altogether. Spiritual growth involves cultivating your character and training your inward being in a positive direction. For the Christian, it means being transformed to reflect the character of Jesus. When you accept Christ as your Savior and enter a relationship with Him, His Spirit gives life to yours and begins to shape your inner nature. Over time, you grow to be more and more like Him.

**Relational**: Relationships are the centerpiece of your life. What you accomplish spiritually, physically, financially, and professionally are but a means to an end. Relationships are that end. Our most important relationship is our relationship with God—that's why the spiritual aspect of our lives is the highest priority—but the nature of that relationship will impact all others. We are social beings created to live in community with families and friends. John Donne wrote, "No man is an island, entire of itself; every man is a piece of the continent, a part of the main." Jesus exhorted His followers to love our neighbors as ourselves, calling it the second great commandment. So your success in life will never far exceed your success in the area of your relationships. To the degree that your relationships thrive, joy and fulfillment will thrive. A Blueprint for Life simply must include a strategy for your relationships.

> **So your success in life will never far exceed your success in the area of your relationships.**

**Physical/Emotional**: Your physical body is the vehicle through which you live out life. It's the "earth suit" that enables you to function in this world. It is also inseparably linked with your emotions. Needless to say, the state of your physical and emotional health can have a tremendous impact on the other areas of your life. Diet, exercise, and medical care and prevention can affect the quality of life and even prolong it. Setting goals in this area is an important part of life planning.

**Financial**: In the Bible, there is more written about money than any other subject—including heaven or hell. In fact, one out of every ten Bible verses is a reference to money, possessions, or some principle that can be applied to the handling of personal property. Not only does your management of money reflect the priorities of your heart, it also affects which directions you're able to follow. It can offer the freedom to pursue opportunities in each of the other four categories or it can limit your potential

> **In the Bible, there is more written about money than any other subject—including heaven or hell.**

as well. The state of your finances says a lot about you. How you spend, save, and invest is a direct reflection of your character and values. Setting financial goals is not only practical; it represents a discipline that will impact the very core of your life.

**Career**: Eight hours a day . . . five days a week . . . 50 weeks a year . . . for 40 years. That adds up to nearly ten years—not including overtime. That's more than a third of your waking life spent at work! If that's a depressing thought, then maybe you should consider setting some goals to improve your professional life. It's important to maximize your enjoyment during the many hours you will spend on the job. Work can and should be rewarding. Your career has the potential to be the primary place where you exercise your God-given talent, wisdom, and skills. This area of your life directly influences everything else about you. It can set the course of your life. It's vital to plan this area wisely.

Now that you have been introduced to "The Big Five," you may recognize that virtually any issue that needs attention in your life will fit squarely into one of these categories. In the next few chapters, we will explore each one these areas and discuss what you'll need to consider as you set goals for each.

A Blueprint for Life calls for a well-designed plan that incorporates specific and unique strategies in each of these five areas. These areas will work in harmony to help you discover the life you were born to live.

*Chapter Seven*

# Your Spiritual Blueprint

*"I am the vine, you are the branches; he who abides in Me and I in him, he bears much fruit, for apart from Me you can do nothing."*

*~ John 15:5*

One of the most critical concepts to understand as we explore the five aspects of your life is that your spiritual condition has more power to determine success or failure than any other area. Your capacity for making good decisions hinges on the condition of your spirit. So when we talk about spiritual goals, we aren't talking about religion. There's a huge difference between outward religious practices and a genuine relationship with God. Spiritual growth involves shaping your character and training your inner being in the direction of God's blueprint for your life.

> **There's a huge difference between outward religious practices and a genuine relationship with God.**

## CREATING YOUR SPIRITUAL BLUEPRINT

God has a blueprint for your spirit, but few people have a clear understanding of what their spirit is. Many think of it as a ghostly entity that we become when we die—that the remnant of our real selves floats around in heaven without any form or substance. The truth is that your spirit is already fully present now. It isn't a remnant; it's the core of who you are. And the idea is to develop it into what God intended when He created you. Simply put, your spirit is what inhabits your physical body and gives it life. It thinks, it feels, it determines your worldview and your perspective, and it shapes your overall demeanor and attitude. *It's the real you.*

In some ways, you can compare yourself to a highly sophisticated fighter jet. It has a body—a fuselage, wings, and a powerful engine. It has a brain—onboard computers and sensitive electronics to analyze flight data and control every ounce of the aircraft with extreme precision. But none of it functions without the pilot. He's like the spirit of the airplane. He operates the controls. He looks at the data and makes decisions. He determines whether the plane is flying a peaceful mission or engaged in an act of war. Likewise, you have a physical body, as well as a brain to analyze data and send messages through your nervous system to control your body. But without the spirit, nobody's home. Your spirit is like the pilot—the decision-maker. It determines what kind of mission you're on.

For example, when you're happy, you're happy in your spirit. And wherever you go, your spirit directs your body to go into "happy" mode. Your countenance and your body language are more energetic and open. Your tone of voice is warm and friendly. You make gestures and speech that reflect your happiness. And when you're sad or angry, that comes from your spirit too. It's as if your spirit flips the "don't mess with me" switch. Your countenance darkens. Your speech may be gruff. And you may notice yourself using gestures that simply don't come from a happy person. Same body, same surroundings, same brain, different spirit.

Your spirit is fully functional apart from your physical body. Paul described it this way:

*"We know that when this tent we live in now is taken down—when we die and leave these bodies—we will have wonderful new bodies in heaven, homes that will be ours forevermore, made for us by God himself and not by human hands. How weary we grow of our present bodies. That is why we look forward eagerly to the day when we shall have heavenly bodies that we shall put on like new clothes. For we shall not be merely spirits without bodies. These earthly bodies make us groan and sigh, but we wouldn't like to think of dying and having no bodies at all. We want to slip into our new bodies so that these dying bodies will, as it were, be swallowed up by everlasting life. This is what God has prepared for us, and as a guarantee he has given us his Holy Spirit. Now we look forward with confidence to our heavenly bodies, realizing that every moment we spend in these earthly bodies is time spent away from our eternal home in heaven with Jesus. We know these things are true by believing, not by seeing. And we are not afraid but are quite content to die, for then we will be at home with the Lord."*

**2 Corinthians 5:1-8 TLB**

So you see, your spirit is not some esoteric entity deep inside you. It's you—your thoughts, your feelings, your person. It's just that you exist inside a body for now. So when we talk about spiritual goals, we're not talking about religion. We're talking about the thinking, walking, talking you, not some ethereal being that comes out and roams the heavens after you die. You're already here—behind your physical costume, inside your brain with its temporary earthly strengths and weaknesses. Beneath it all is a person. And your outward physical expressions and mannerisms give a very accurate depiction of what kind of spirit you are. Eternity has already begun; it's just that the first phase takes place in your current body.

The spiritual component is arguably the most important of the five areas of life. Not only is it the part of you that will live forever, but it's also the foundation for all other areas. Much of what happens in your finances, career, relationships, and physical life is a direct reflection of the decisions you make in your spirit. This is where your success or failure in the rest of your life will come from. It's where your decisions are made. That's why a strategy for your spiritual life is absolutely essential. Like a muscle, your spirit either grows or atrophies. You

> **Much of what happens in your finances, career, relationships, and physical life is a direct reflection of the decisions you make in your spirit.**

can't grow spiritually without God's power working within you, but you still have to be intentional about growing. It won't just happen passively. You have the capacity to determine how you will grow and how you will allow yourself to be shaped in the direction of God's blueprint for your life.

## DEVOTIONAL LIFE

You were created for fellowship with God. In fact, the whole world was designed as a stage for that relationship. The land and sea . . . countries . . . industry . . . families . . . life and all its governing principles . . . all are a backdrop for the main event—your relationship with Him. So the more you cultivate that relationship and align yourself with God and His way of thinking, the more you align yourself with the way things work in the world. Following God's principles for your finances will lead to better financial success. Knowing His ideas about relationships will help your family. The same is true in the workplace, in the neighborhood—wherever you go. And it all goes back to the cornerstone relationship: you and God.

*"Take my yoke upon you and learn from me, for I am gentle and humble*

*in heart, and you will find rest for your souls. For my yoke is easy and my
burden is light."*

**Matthew 11:29-30 NIV**

*"I am the good shepherd; I know my sheep and my sheep know me."*

**John 10:14 NIV**

*"Yes, I am the Vine; you are the branches. Whoever lives in me and I in him
shall produce a large crop of fruit. For apart from me you can't do a thing."*

**John 15:5 TLB**

That's why spiritual goals are not about religion. A spiritual relationship
with God is a relationship involving you, the person. And it touches every
part of your life. It can't be compartmentalized.

Your devotional life is vital to your spiritual life. This is your focused
time with God—for prayer, Bible reading, and getting personal with Him.
You should have strategic goals for this area of your life. Some of these
goals may be hard to define, and you may need to adjust them pretty fre-
quently, as spiritual growth is hard to measure. But how much time do
you spend talking with Him? In what ways would you like to see Him
show up in your life? How effective do you want your prayer life to be?
How well do you want to know the Bible? In what ways would you like
to impact other people spiritually? How
do you want to serve Him? When you
think of the fruit of the Spirit—according to Galatians 5:22, that fruit includes
love, joy, peace, patience, kindness, goodness, faithfulness, gentleness, and self-

> **Fellowship with
> God must be your
> HIGHEST priority in
> life.**

control—which ones need the greatest growth in your life? What sins, habits, or other hindrances to your relationship with God do you need to overcome? Do you want to be known as a loving, forgiving, grateful person? What degree of spiritual power and maturity do you want to walk in? These are questions you will want to consider when developing your spiritual blueprint.

These things don't just happen by accident. Yes, God is orchestrating your life to develop you spiritually—the experiences you go through and obstacles you overcome aren't random—but you need to be spiritually proactive and prepared as you make choices and respond to what God is doing. And to a greater degree than we're inclined to think, our experience of God is determined by our hunger for Him. How much do you desire His presence? What kind of persistence do you have as you pursue a deeper relationship with Him? God is a rewarder of those who diligently seek Him (Hebrews 11:6), so seeking matters. These responses—hunger and persistence—are the conditions that can determine the quality of your devotional life and your spiritual growth. When God sees these qualities in His people, He makes sure they find Him and grow deeper with Him.

> **God is a rewarder of those who diligently seek Him (Hebrews 11:6), so seeking matters.**

While hungering for God's presence and persistently seeking Him will motivate you and keep you going spiritually, there are practical steps you can take to put yourself in a position to grow. Remember that the best way to accomplish a huge goal is to take baby steps to get there. If you've never had a devotional time, for example, perhaps it would be reasonable to try a baby step to get you started—maybe five minutes when you wake up each morning. The time you spend in your relationship with God will bring greater returns than any other investment of your time you could make. If you know that you need to be a more forgiving person—that bitterness is dragging you down—choose one person who has offended you in the past and simply forgive that person this week. Most of all, ask God to help you get where you need to be. The first answer to any spiritual issue is simply to ask Him. He will certainly respond to your desire to grow.

As you develop your spiritual goals, remember that a focus on yourself can be a hindrance. Our goal is to focus on God, to grow in our connection with His heart, to learn how to relate to Him. In many ways, this is about accomplishing goals, but in many ways it isn't. He is the goal. How can your blueprint reflect the objective of gaining a deeper understanding of who God is? What are His likes and dislikes? What is your ongoing strategy for learning about Him? Once you prioritize Him, all other priorities fall in place much easily.

> **How can your blueprint reflect the objective of gaining a deeper understanding of who God is?**

## CHURCH

The Bible emphasizes involvement with other believers. This gives you an opportunity to receive blessings as well as to serve and be a blessing to others. You'll need to set specific goals in this area as well. What level of church involvement should you pursue? What leadership role might you play? Which areas of church service interest you the most? How can you pray for and support the spiritual leaders within your sphere of influence? Are there any key relationships that would be beneficial? Perhaps finding a mentor or surrounding yourself with people who can give you wise counsel can help you recognize when you're on track and when you aren't. Or maybe you should consider being a mentor to someone else. It's often said that everyone should have relationships that feed them spiritually and those in which they feed others. These are the types of issues you should consider as you plan this area of your life.

## DISCOVERING YOUR SPIRITUAL GIFTS

In setting goals for your church involvement and your relationships with believers, it's important to understand your spiritual gifts. Every person has specific talents and gifts. We're each equipped for special purposes in order to perform certain duties in support of God's agenda. We're born with many of these gifts—things we're naturally good at doing. But when we accept Christ and are filled with His Spirit, we're also given

> **Every person has specific talents and gifts. We're each equipped for special purposes in order to perform certain duties in support of God's agenda.**

spiritual gifts. These are abilities that are empowered by the Spirit Himself. They may or may not overlap with our natural talents. Someone who is not a naturally gifted speaker, for example, could have a spiritual gift of teaching and powerfully impact others by getting up and instructing people in biblical truth. Or someone who is not naturally very persuasive could carry quite a bit of influence whenever he or she shares the gospel message. Sometimes it's easy to pick up on a person's spiritual gifts, and sometimes it isn't until you see them operating in those gifts. But everyone has at least one.

If you don't know what your spiritual gifts are, you'll want to spend some time asking God to show you. You may also want to take a spiritual gift "inventory"—there are several offered by churches and found on web sites that ask a series of questions to help you discover what God is empowering you to do. Usually you realize your areas of giftedness as you serve God in various capacities. Some tasks will come easily to you or result in spiritual fruit in others, while some may seem difficult. If you feel like God is blowing wind in your sails as you teach, serve, give, pray for things that require unusual faith, or perform any other spiritual service, that's probably evidence of a spiritual gift. Or, if your service seems uneventful to you but you notice unusual response to it or effectiveness in its results, that's probably evidence of giftedness too. On the other hand, if certain acts of service seem like walking through mud and result in very little fruit, you probably aren't gifted in that area. That doesn't mean you have no responsibility there—all Christians are called to encourage, evangelize, pray in faith, be hospitable, etc., whether they have special empowerment from God in these areas or not. But you will want to give special emphasis and invest most of your time in the areas in which you are most gifted.

## THE SPIRITUAL LIFE YOU WERE BORN TO LIVE

**Your spiritual growth is the most important part of your existence. It can't be separated from other areas; rather, it impacts every aspect of who you are.**

The more you understand about yourself, the better you can leverage your God-given strengths to serve God during your time on earth. As you examine this aspect of your life and set goals for it, keep in mind that God has a blueprint for your spiritual life. He is preparing you to accomplish your mission and to bear spiritual fruit that will last forever.

Your spiritual growth is the most important part of your existence. It can't be separated from other areas; rather, it impacts every aspect of who you are.

Remember that your spiritual growth is not a mold that's identical to that of other Christians. You are an individual, uniquely designed to relate to God in particular ways and to represent His nature and His purposes in a way that others can't do. He wants a very personal relationship with you, marked by unique encounters that reflect your personality and His. Spiritual disciplines like Bible study, prayer, and worship are not meant to be activities to check off your list. He doesn't want you to develop a relationship with activities or principles—even good, biblical ones. He wants to lead you not by formulas but by communicating with you constantly. But even developing your blueprint is a form of communication with Him. And these disciplines are time-tested venues for experiencing Him. As you implement them, keep your heart focused on God Himself. And His plans for your spiritual growth will begin to take shape and develop you into the person He designed you to be.

*Chapter Eight*

# Your Relationships Blueprint

*"The things you eat, the place you work, the clothes you wear, the car you drive—all of these are merely costumes and stage props for the main event—relationships."*

*~ Anonymous*

## THE MAIN EVENT

You were created for relationships. In the beginning, God created human beings to have fellowship with Him—the first relationship. While
Adam was still learning his way around the garden, God created Eve to
be his partner, one person with another. And ever since, God has been
intensely interested in the relationships between people. Five of the Ten
Commandments give instructions about interacting with others. Many of
Jesus' parables revolved around personal relationships and how they should
be conducted. Throughout history, most of God's will for the world has
been carried out through the relational activities of people. And when it
came time for the grand climax of His interaction with humanity, the me-
dium God chose was a personal relationship—Jesus in the flesh, walking
and talking with men and women.

We can learn to be happy without money. Our joy can survive almost any
physical condition or career situation, but take away relationships—or the
hope of them—and we will soon lose our will to live. It's no coincidence
that solitary confinement has earned its place as one of the most-used
instruments of torture. Next to food, water, and oxygen, our need for con-

necting with others ranks as the highest basic necessity. You can't create a life blueprint without including a strategy for developing and maintaining the important relationships in your life.

After your spiritual development, this is the most important area of your blueprint. When all is said and done, the strength of your relationships will determine your level of joy at the finish. It's possible to amass wealth and still be miserable. You can achieve every career goal and yet be unfulfilled. You can be the picture of health and still feel empty inside. But rare is the person who reaches old age with a portfolio of rich relationships and doesn't feel joy and elation. Naked we come from the womb, and naked we return. But the relationships we encounter along the way are the very currency of eternity.

> **Naked we come from the womb, and naked we return. But the relationships we encounter along the way are the very currency of eternity.**

The things you eat, the clothes you wear, the car you drive—all of these are merely the costumes and stage props for the main event—relationships. Therefore, relationships should be a priority when making your blueprint.

## YOUR RELATIONSHIP PORTFOLIO

Everyone has a "relationship portfolio." There are many different types of relationships in your portfolio: spouse, family, friends, co-workers, neighbors, etc. For Christians, the portfolio often contains additional relationships that can play a role in achieving your goals: pastor, mentor, disciples, accountability partners, fellowship groups, and more. Depending on how well these relationships function, they can either support your pursuit of your purpose in life or detract from it.

As you create a blueprint for your relationships, you may conclude that certain key relationships are missing from your life. Likewise, you might decide to scale back on some of the relationships that aren't central to your purpose in life. As a good steward of the time God has given you, you should be intentional about cultivating the right balance of relationships to enable your life purpose—whether that means creating new relationships in key categories where they don't exist yet or allowing nonessential relationships to expire.

> As a good steward of the time God has given you, you should be intentional about cultivating the right balance of relationships to enable your life purpose.

## TIME AND ENVIRONMENTS

Two concepts are particularly important for cultivating the key relationships in your portfolio: time and environments. All relationships require an investment of time, and all take place in an environment. The amount and quality of each of these components will determine the health of the relationship.

## TIME

There are many ways to express love to someone. You can buy gifts. You can give compliments. You can give a pat on the back or a heartfelt smile. All of these are valid expressions of love. But nothing speaks louder to the priority of a relationship than the amount of time you are willing to invest in that person. That's why love has been spelled T - I - M - E. The depth of a relationship is directly proportional to the time you put into it. A husband can call home, send flowers, mail cards, and make promises, but if he never comes home from work, his wife knows exactly where his priorities lie. In the same way, you can buy expensive toys for your child or send him to the greatest camps and playgrounds in the world, but if you don't spend an adequate amount of time with him, the relationship will suffer.

Quality of time is important too, not just quantity. When someone feels like a priority, bonds strengthen. When the relationship is short-changed, it suffers. *Which* time you carve out for somebody should fit the priority you give that relationship.

Friendships need time to allow bonds to develop. And special relationships need time because it expresses love and builds intimacy. Your most important relationships should get top priority when setting goals and making plans.

## ENVIRONMENTS

*Where you go* can say a lot about *who you're with*. A fast-food lunch is one thing, but dinner at a nice restaurant usually conveys something more about the value of the relationship. Regular, everyday contact and a casual atmosphere can be an important foundation. But special, planned outings can be an opportunity to be strategic about making the relationship what you want it to be. This may not apply to every relationship. And you can't always control it. But when you're thinking of strategies for various relationships, it's definitely something to keep in mind.

## SPECIFIC STRATEGIES

Each type of relationship will require a different approach. So let's look at a few of them to see what they require, and how you might make them more strategic:

> **Next to your relationship with God, there's no relationship more important than the one with your spouse.**

*Spouse*: Next to your relationship with God, there's no relationship more important than the one with your spouse. The Bible says that a man's wife is like his own flesh, and it instructs him to live sacrificially for her. It also calls wives to a level of devotion toward their husbands that is beyond any other human relationship. Your spouse is your first ministry. This relationship is the foundation for all other relationships after it. To the degree that it thrives, your other relationships are free to thrive as well. If there's a deficit in your relationship with your spouse, it will trickle down to affect all the others. If you're going to examine the priorities of your relationships, this is the place to start.

There is something unromantic about the idea of being strategic with a love relationship, at least on the surface. No one wants a romance to unfold and grow methodically. An exciting relationship with your spouse involves feelings of emotions and spontaneity. But a long-term, healthy, thriving relationship requires a certain level of planning. Anyone can fall in love, but it takes work to stay that way. Do you have a plan for being in love in 10 years . . . 20 . . . 50? Being strategic doesn't mean taking the spice out of your relationship. It means making sure there's plenty of spice to last the whole way.

So how do you put your wife or husband first? What kinds of things should you consider when making strategies for this area?

> **Anyone can fall in love, but it takes work to stay that way.**

Start with time and environments. The calendar doesn't lie. Do the amount and priority of time spent together fit your goals for long-term intimacy? Do you have a strategy for spending quality time with your spouse? Should you cultivate more environments where the relationship will thrive? Do you have regular dates together? Do you have a plan for getting away for the weekend—or longer? As you imagine yourself one day looking back over your life together, what key experiences would you not want to miss? Are there special places you'd like to go? Things you'd like to do? Identify the landmark experiences for your marriage and begin now to make a plan to ensure they happen.

Landmark events are one thing. But the quality of life along the way is even more important. Are there any day-to-day things you should consider? Do you ever have devotional time together? Do you remember to ask, "How was your day?" And do you stop and truly listen when he or she gives the answer? Do you take walks? Trips without the kids? Unexpected phone calls during the day?

What do you need to do to express your love for your spouse—to make him or her feel loved? Do you know how to recognize your spouse's "love language"? Does receiving a gift hit the spot? Or do words of affirmation go much further? Perhaps visible acts of service around your household say "I love you" best: unloading the dishwasher, vacuuming the carpet, doing yard work, or taking out the trash.

Are you sensitive to your spouse's needs? Do you have a plan for recognizing ways to serve him or her? What are his or her personal desires? Do you need more romantic gestures? Is the level of physical intimacy where you both want it? Are there chores left undone? Would he or she benefit from a night out with a close friend (other than you)? These are just a few things you can do to meet the personal needs of your spouse.

When you look back on your life together, no relationship will have been more pivotal than that with your spouse. If you aren't strategic in this area, you very well may be disappointed with the outcome. At the same time, a little planning and a little foresight can not only avoid potential pitfalls, but can also make a good relationship truly great.

## CHILDREN

The Bible calls children a blessing—an inheritance from the Lord. Your relationships with them should reflect this perspective. But a truly rich relationship with a child takes special insight. A child's communication skills are still developing. He is less likely to tell you when he requires love and attention. He may not even understand his own feelings and needs. Even if he appears outspoken and content, there may be hidden voids below the surface. So it's up to the parent to make sure the relationship is rich and deep.

> **So how can you make your child feel loved and appreciated? Individual time is a good place to start.**

So how can you make your child feel loved and appreciated? Individual time is a good place to start—a father-daughter date night, a father-son "boys' night," or a special mother-child outing. It doesn't have to cost a lot or require much planning. An impromptu day off work to spend together on a bike ride or a hike can become an indelible, lifetime memory. Even little moments out of the daily routine—racing cars on the floor, sharing a bedtime story, helping with a building-block project—can go a long way toward showing your love and attention. As children grow, the activities change. But as long as you are showing interest in the interests of your child, you are demonstrating appreciation and helping him or her feel loved.

Structured activities give opportunities to step into your child's world. Coaching the little league team or just cheering from the sidelines . . . attending school programs and piano recitals . . . time together in Bible study . . . hobbies shared together . . . bedtime routines . . . all of these can help lay a foundation for rewarding relationships. And of course, love should also be communicated in words, letters/cards, notes in the lunch box, and a frequent verbal "I love you."

## PARENTS

As an adult, your relationship with your parents can prove to be one of the most rewarding—or challenging. Or it can fade and slip by without your realizing it. Even if you feel pain or anger, you are commanded to honor them. While you're busy building a career and raising a family of your own, you need to be proactive about spending time and expressing love to your parents. A few suggestions include: vacations together, Sunday dinners, frequent phone calls, letters/cards, gifts, impromptu visits, time alone together (with and with-

> **While you're busy building a career and raising a family of your own, you need to be proactive about spending time and expressing love to your parents.**

out the grandchildren), and shared hobbies like sports, shopping, sewing, or golf. And of course, *now* is the time to say, "I love you."

## FRIENDS

Friendships are important for everyone. From constructive friendships like mentors or accountability partners to those that are just plain fun. Some people are naturally relational and never lack company. Others will have to work at it. If you tend to have plenty of friends, the focus will be on selecting your friendships wisely and making sure they have purpose. If you tend to keep to yourself, you may need to focus on stepping out and developing the right kinds of friendships. Either way, you need to be strategic and choose relationships that are vital to your mission and overall goals. If you don't, you'll simply drift.

Friendships tend to form around common interests, or comfort zones. We are naturally pulled toward environments and people that help us feel accepted. As a result, we can end up in relationships that may serve an emotional need or longing but are not necessarily strategic to our mission statement. That doesn't mean we should use people strategically for our own purposes; friendships need to be much more natural and personal than that. But we can avoid relationships that don't build us up, that drain us of time and energy, or that pull us away from our calling. The challenge is to begin considering the purpose of the relationships that you allow into your life—to begin intentionally pursuing relationships that support your life purpose and avoiding those that don't.

You'll need to ask God for discernment about which relationships enhance your calling and which ones don't. Avoid limiting your relationships to a narrow circle of friends that think and act like you do. You'll want some close friendships with people you can confide in, of course—people with whom you can be vulnerable, who are not reluctant to be honest with you and give you straightforward counsel. That probably means people you've known for a while and with whom you have a certain level of trust. But you'll also want to expand your vision to include people outside your normal circles—to meet new friends. You're called to make disciples, and that happens most naturally within authentic friendships. Allow people into your life who need the spiritual gifts and insights you have to offer. Make an effort to pursue some relationships that reach out in addition to cultivating the ones you already have.

So ask yourself: Are your friendships fulfilling and fun? Are they constructive? Being selective doesn't mean you can't have any casual friendships that don't meet a specific goal. This doesn't mean you have to get rid of all your friends and start over. But you may want to make some tough decisions about how you spend your time. Some people will need to eliminate some relationships completely—not to be mean or unfriendly, but to serve a greater goal. This may require doing some things that feel awkward or unnatural. But the end goal is to develop the types of relationships that will help you to fulfill your mission and purpose. If you begin to analyze and evaluate relationships based on their purpose, you'll find that your overall life experience is more rewarding.

> **The end goal is to develop the types of relationships that will help you to fulfill your mission and purpose.**

## THE RELATIONSHIPS YOU WERE BORN TO DISCOVER

Remember, God has an ideal plan for each and every relationship in your life. They aren't always easy, but the ones God has called you to develop can be full of purpose and meaning. Your closest relationships can be some of the most fulfilling gifts God has ever given you. As you gain wisdom about relationships from scripture, you can begin to develop a blueprint that will give you guidance for cultivating the ones you are called to experience in your life.

*Chapter Nine*

# Your Physical Blueprint

*"Therefore, I urge you, brothers, in view of God's mercy, to offer your bodies as living sacrifices, holy and pleasing to God—this is your spiritual act of worship."*

*~ Romans 12:1*

The God-given vision of the life you were born to live also includes a picture of the body you were meant to live in. A lot of people so emphasize the importance of the spirit that they neglect the body as a relatively unimportant aspect of life. But scripture is clear that our bodies matter. God gave them to us for a reason. Our physical condition and chemical balance can profoundly affect our moods, our relationships, and our decisions. When we don't take good care of our bodies, we risk negatively affecting every other area of our lives.

"Your body is a temple of the Holy Spirit," we are told. "You are not your own; you were bought with a price. Therefore honor God with your body" (1 Corinthians 6:19-20). From your spiritual pursuits to your material ones, your body is the container that will carry you through life. How you maintain it is an integrity issue. Paul tells us to offer our bodies as living sacrifices that are holy and pleasing to God (Romans 12:1). It belongs to Him and can be offered to Him as an act of worship. Your whole physical being is meant to help you carry out God's mission in this world, so developing a physical blueprint is relevant to your blueprint for every other area of your life.

## CHECKING UNDER THE HOOD

Imagine you are going on a trip. This is not just any trip; it's the family vacation of a lifetime. The car is packed. The route is planned. The reservations are made. Everything is in place. As your family members fasten their seatbelts and break out the games, anticipation fills the air. But as you turn on the motor, something else begins to fill the air: smoke. The thick, blue kind that looks like it won't clear up by itself. Next, you hear a loud rattling sound from under the hood. Finally, there's a horrendous moan of grinding metal and the engine stops. Silence. Vacation over.

Your body is a vehicle. It's your primary means of transportation everywhere you go. If you neglect it, abuse it, or overuse it, the trip will have detours. Or worse. You can have the most meticulous plans for your life, but if you don't have a plan for taking care of your body, you could end up on the side of the road. The whole reason you need physical goals is to make sure you have the vehicle to carry out your God-given mission in life.

> **The whole reason you need physical goals is to make sure you have the vehicle to carry out your God-given mission in life.**

So how closely does that person in the mirror resemble the person you've dreamed of being? We're not talking about winning a beauty contest, pursuing worldly vanity, or signing up for an extreme makeover. But inside each of us is a vision for the fitness level, medical health, and general appearance we will need to live out our purpose in life. The blueprint you create will help move you toward that vision.

How you maintain your physical body may seem like a peripheral issue, but it's really a matter of integrity. Laziness and poor stewardship in this area are almost always an indication of laziness and poor stewardship in other areas. We can't control everything about our physical condition, but when we don't treat our bodies like "a temple of the Holy Spirit" (1 Corinthians 6:19), it makes a statement about our character.

## Physical Goals

When God created human beings, He could have made us any way He wanted. He could have made us all look the same—distinguishable only by our names or maybe our voices. He could have made us so we never needed food or sleep. He could have created us so we didn't have human bodies at all . . . like a version of the angels. But He didn't. For whatever reason, God created each one of us the way we are with each of our unique features. He created us with a need for nourishment, sleep, and physical activity. Your life blueprint should acknowledge and address these facts.

Paul wrote that your body is a temple of the Holy Spirit. From your spiritual pursuits to your earthly ones, your body is the vessel that carries you. It's your "earth suit," and it needs to last. The container isn't as important as the contents, but it can affect everything about them. If the seal is broken on a bottle of medicine, the instructions say, "Do not use." If canned foods become punctured, the contents can quickly spoil and become toxic. In the same way, your physical state can alter the state of everything else— your finances, your work, your relationships . . . even your spiritual life. And when you get sick, you cancel all other plans and go home. Here are five key areas you'll want to include when setting physical goals:

*Exercise/Fitness*: Your body was created for physical activity. It thrives on it. Exercise can stimulate the functionality of every system in your body:

cardiovascular, nervous, immune, and digestive. Exercise can improve your strength and flexibility, preventing injuries, increasing stamina, and equipping you to thrive at daily tasks. But that's not all. Exercise also addresses self-esteem issues related to your physical appearance.

Consistency and frequency are the keys to fitness. Your plan should include a strategy for weekly exercise routines, as well as specific goals to measure your accomplishments—maximum weight lifted, distance run, proficiency achieved at a particular sport, etc. You can also include goals for your body weight, and a plan in the event you exceed your weight range. Do you desire goals for clothing size, waist size, or muscle tone? Write them down and measure your progress from time to time. And consider recruiting your spouse or a friend as a workout partner. The accountability will greatly improve your chances for staying consistent.

If you're not sure where to start, consider joining an exercise class or hiring a personal trainer for a period. Guides for basic exercise programs can also be found in your local library or on the Internet. And as always, consult your doctor before beginning any exercise program.

Also, if there are any habits that affect your life, you may want to devise a strategy for those. Smoking, nail-biting, substance abuse . . . whatever the challenge, if it impairs your vision and plan for your life, it warrants addressing in your physical blueprint.

*Diet:* Just like a car needs gas, your body needs fuel. But that's not all. Different organs and systems need specific vitamins and minerals to perform properly. Even if you keep your stomach full, you could still be starving your body of vital nutrients it needs to function. For most people, there's no need to go overboard here. Most doctors recommend that a basic, balanced diet of the four food groups is adequate. Supplemental vitamins can help but are not a substitute for just plain eating right. For your digestive system, the act of processing roughage and absorbing nutrients from food's bio-matter seems to be just as beneficial as the actual food itself. That's the only exercise it gets.

Your goals should include a plan for learning and understanding some basic dietary facts. Can you name the four food groups? Do you know the recommended portions for each one? Do you know what kinds of foods to avoid? A quick read at the library or on the Internet might be all you need to begin mastering the basics. Some people choose to monitor the size or frequency of meals. Is there a relationship between the nutritional value when you dine out versus when you eat at home? If so, you might want a plan for that. Dietary goals can be unique for each individual, so you should personalize them accordingly.

*Sleep*: Just like your body needs exercise, it also needs rest. The National Sleep Foundation conducted a survey of 1,004 Americans and learned that the vast majority—63 percent—do not get the eight hours recommended by experts for good health. As much as 40 percent indicated that they are so sleepy during the day that it interferes with their daily activities several times a month. Nearly half reported that they have driven while drowsy, and 20 percent say they have actually fallen asleep while behind the wheel.

> **Somewhere along the way, we have lost the perception that sleep is a necessity for good health, and we tend to consider it a negotiable or a luxury instead.**

Somewhere along the way, we have lost the perception that sleep is a necessity for good health, and we tend to consider it a negotiable or a luxury instead. If you want good health and optimal performance—whether achieving at work or just staying awake during your prayer time—you need a strategy for getting a good night's sleep. You should set a time for going to bed and work your schedule back from there. People's sleep needs can vary. So you might do well to have a certain number of hours as a goal. Pay attention to the impact that certain foods and drinks can have on restful sleep—and the way evening snacks can alter sleep patterns.

*Medical strategy:* There's no way to overstate the impact preventive medicine can have on both the length and quality of your life. Regular checkups not only avert potential problems, they can also provide peace-of-mind and present opportunities for improving your health and wellbeing.

An annual physical is the first place to start. Most experts agree that a yearly overview offers a good interval for spotting potential problems early and keeping track of immunizations, tetanus boosters, and the like. In addition, age-related screenings are recommended for various points in life. These include important tests such as mammograms and colon or prostate exams beginning at age 40. Your doctor can tell you the checkpoints that apply to you.

In addition to preventive and responsive medicine, there may be elective procedures to consider. For example, outpatient eye surgery can eliminate the need for glasses or contacts for some people. Immunotherapy (allergy shots) can alleviate or eliminate unwanted seasonal or perpetual allergy symptoms. There are procedures to repair hindered air passages, helping you breathe better and warding off illness. Damaged or worn-out joints can sometimes benefit from physical therapy or surgical techniques. Would any of these procedures enable you to fulfill your purpose in life better? Ask your doctor to help you assess your level of need and develop a recommendation. Then incorporate it into your overall Blueprint for Life.

*Appearance*: Appearance is important to your self-esteem. Some people might say that's superficial, but it's true for almost everyone. Though we live in a narcissistic world that emphasizes physical attractiveness, we aren't talking about developing a life that's only skin-deep. This isn't about finding your identity or your value as a person in superficialities. But being confident in your appearance doesn't have to imply vanity. Clearly you shouldn't pursue vanity, but neither should you neglect the basics of personal appearance. We've already addressed body weight and muscle tone, but there are other points to consider as well.

First of all, have you ever thought about how your overall appearance affects your calling and purpose in life? Do you have an overriding goal that's appropriate for your other objectives? What kind of physical condition will best support you? Does appearance matter at all? Whether you are a professional model, a salesperson, a homemaker, or a policeman wearing a uniform, your unique place in life brings with it unique requirements related to appearance.

Next, what about your wardrobe? Are there certain types of outfits that you want to be sure are up-to-date to aid your career goals or your relationship goals? Are there some areas that are less important in which you could cut back and save money? Do you have a plan for refreshing your wardrobe? Does it take advantage of seasonal sales and discount prices?

If certain appearance items will help you fulfill your purpose in life, it might be worth the additional effort. As you seek God's kingdom first, the pure desires of your heart will begin to emerge, revealing a picture of the physical body you should pursue for yourself.

*Mental/Emotional*: Just as your physical condition affects your performance, your mental and emotional state also has the ability to propel you toward your goals or leave you stranded on the side of the road. For some people, emotions rarely warrant a second thought. But for an increasing number of people, mental or emotional hindrances can be quite debilitating. Virtually everyone, if they examine it enough, can identify an area or two to make improvements and find increased freedom and a better quality of life.

> **Just as your physical condition affects your performance, your mental and emotional state also has the ability to propel you toward your goals or leave you stranded on the side of the road.**

From person to person, the range of possibilities in this category is diverse. So only a self-assessment can determine what steps you may want to include in your life blueprint. For example, an ordinary fear of flying is not uncommon. But if it causes you to avoid certain trips or pass up opportunities that serve your overall purpose, you might want to develop a strategy for overcoming that fear. The same is true of stage fright, fear of crowds, fear of driving, etc. We are fortunate to live in a time when effective treatments are available for even the most significant phobias, panic disorders, and clinical depression.

So are there any fears that might be limiting your potential? Are there painful or unpleasant memories from the past that haven't been fully reconciled? Has an experience involving your past left you with any trace of guilt or shame? Would you be a happier, more productive person if you could rid those feelings once and for all? If you desire a strategy for overcoming any of these limitations, chances are that help is readily available.

## DISCOVERING THE PHYSICAL BODY YOU WERE BORN TO LIVE IN

**How can having a healthy body help you accomplish God's purpose for your life?**

Ask yourself some questions that will help you develop a blueprint for your physical life. How can having a healthy body help you accomplish God's purpose for your life? Just as temporal resources like time and money can be leveraged for eternal purposes, in what ways can your physical body be leveraged for eternal purposes? How does your physical well-being affect your attitudes? Your decisions? Your relationships? What steps can you take to make sure you are physically healthy and balanced? What baby steps can you take this week to continue on the road to health? Remember, your body's main function is to serve as the vehicle for accomplishing God's purpose for your life. Keep this in mind as you set your goals.

*Chapter Ten*

# Your Financial Blueprint

*"He is no fool who gives what he cannot keep to gain what he cannot lose."*

*~ Jim Elliot*

As we work hard to earn money to provide for our basic needs and fund our desired lifestyle, we tend to forget that God is the true owner of our possessions. "Everything under the heaven and the earth is yours, O Lord" (1 Chronicles 29:11). "The earth is the Lord's, and everything in it, the world, and all who live in it" (Psalm 24:1). "'The silver is mine and the gold is mine,' declares the Lord Almighty" (Haggai 2:8). These are but a few of the many biblical passages that insist that God owns everything. He made it all, and even our own lives belong to Him. Our ability to earn wealth comes from Him; He gives us the skills and opportunities for us to earn it. We are not owners. Instead, we are stewards. A steward is someone who takes care of another's possessions, doing with them as the owner desires. Whatever God gives us is our responsibility to manage for Him. He entrusts us with money and gives us the opportunity to use it for His purposes.

> **Whatever God gives us is our responsibility to manage for Him. He entrusts us with money and gives us the opportunity to use it for His purposes.**

God did not intend for us to serve money; He meant for money to serve us. In fact, those who spend their lives chasing after money eventually find themselves terribly dissatisfied. When we make money our objective, we discover the truth of what scripture says—that it's like chasing after the wind. It doesn't last, and it can't fulfill us. Sooner or later, we will part ways with our treasure. It will be spent or lose its value or be stolen; or we will die and leave it behind. As we're often reminded, we can't take it with us when we go. That's the truth that makes Jim Elliot's statement, which we quoted earlier, so simply powerful: "He is no fool who gives what he cannot keep to gain what he cannot lose." When we invest our earthly treasure, which we can't keep, and leverage it for treasure in God's kingdom, which we can't lose, we are being very wise.

God calls us to use money as a tool to store up treasures for ourselves in heaven by investing in our life purpose and calling (Matthew 6:20). So much of our focus around money deals with daily provisions on this earth that we often don't stop to think about how well we're investing in our eternal portfolio. But we are called to be generous people and to find great blessing when give and invest in God's kingdom. Much of that blessing may come in this age, but whether it does or not, it certainly comes in heaven. Even though we can't take our money with us, we can, in a very real sense, send it on ahead by investing worldly wealth in eternal purposes. Our treasure in heaven can never be lost, stolen, corrupted, diminished, or exhausted. It is more precious than all the gold and diamonds the world can offer.

## THE REAL VALUE OF A DOLLAR

Achieving your God-given purpose is a life-long process of conforming yourself to the vision God had in mind when He first created you. As we've discussed, He has a plan for your spiritual growth, your relationships, and your physical maintenance. But when it comes to your finances, God's plan focuses less on money itself and more on your attitudes about money. You see, as a Christian you will face all varieties of financial circumstances. And while it's not always within your power to control the level of your income or the stock market, it is within your power to determine your attitudes about the money you possess. In eternity, you will be judged by your attitudes and faithfulness with whatever amount you receive on earth. The real value of money is its ability to reveal what's in our hearts.

There is a tension between the way our world tells us to view our finances and the way God tells us to view them. If we fail to conform to God's plan for our finances—especially how we view money—we will be empty and unfulfilled inside. In order to efficiently use the money God gives you and leverage it for eternity, you will need to create a financial blueprint designed not only to cultivate godly attitudes about money but also to support your God-given purpose in life.

## MONEY DEFINED

There's something about money that strikes a chord with people and touches us personally. Its power has the potential to open wide the door of opportunity or to leave us struggling for our most basic provisions. And just about everyone has an opinion about it. To some, it makes the world go 'round. To others, it is the root of all kinds of evil. And as Jesus cautioned, we all have the potential to serve it like a master.

There's more written about money in the Bible than any other subject—including heaven or hell. One out of every ten Bible verses is a reference to money, possessions, or some principle that can be applied to the handling of personal property. So needless to say, money is a subject that's important to God.

But exactly what is money? How do we define it? Is it a piece of paper? A ticket to personal happiness? Something to hoard for protection and security? Simply put, money is a tool for carrying out God's will. Just like personal skills or

> **Simply put, money is a tool for carrying out God's will.**

life opportunities, money is to be used to bring glory to God and to help us fulfill the call of Ephesians 2:10, to walk in the good works that God has prepared for us beforehand. The first step to embracing this concept of money is the realization that all money—including ours—belongs to God. As stewards rather than owners, we take care of His possessions, using them however He wants us to.

When God blesses you with money or possessions, He has specific things in mind for you to do with it. In order to devise a plan for your money, you must first understand God's will for your money.

## Money's Four Purposes

We can think of many things to do with our money. We can spend it, save it, pay bills, entertain ourselves, spend it on others, and more. Some are godly uses of money. Others can be purely self-indulgent and even harmful. By God's design, money is to serve four main purposes. They are Giving, Provisions, Abundance, and Offerings.

*Giving*: The first reason God gives us money is so we can give it right back to Him in the form of a tithe. Tithe literally means "tenth." God calls us to give of the "first fruits" of our harvest. So we are to give a tenth of our money to God's work by supporting our local church, missions, and other ministries that carry out God's kingdom work. Tithing is a tangible

> **Tithing is a tangible way of acknowledging God as not only the source but also the priority when it comes to our money.**

way of acknowledging God as not only the source but also the priority when it comes to our money.

Remember, you have an eternal portfolio that needs to be funded during your lifetime. Just as you plan for your 401(k), you also need a plan to store up treasure in heaven. The tithe is your basic foundation for eternity.

Giving goes well beyond a monetary tithe, of course. The tithe combined with offerings (see below) is the financial evidence of a life dedicated to God. When we give our treasures, our time, and our talents in His service—from a comprehensive attitude of giving, not just as a percentage of our income—we are well on the way to finding fulfillment. When we act as a reservoir of God's gifts, we find that we don't enjoy them or experience them in abundance. But when we act as a conduit of those gifts, we find that He continues to flow His resources into us because we have been faithful in letting them flow out of us. Financially, this begins with the tithe as a starting point and expands to greater opportunities to sow seeds into His kingdom.

*Provisions*: Another reason God gives us money is to provide for our basic needs. We need food, clothing, shelter, and many other things to live and carry out God's will for our lives. Jesus promised that when your life is committed to God's work, He will take care of all your earthly needs (Matthew 6:33). One way He fulfills this promise is through the money He provides. So it's God's will for you to spend a portion of your money to buy food, clothes, a place to stay, and other basic necessities related to your daily life.

Paying off debt also falls under the category of provision. It's God's will that we be indebted to no one. So when we use money to repay a loan—whether from a past need or an unwise decision—God is providing a way for us to achieve the goal of eliminating debt. Similarly, the Bible advises us to save in preparation for needs to come. Saving is a way of meeting those needs. Investments and savings accounts, from God's perspective, are simply provisions for future needs. Finally, how much you spend on your provisions is a matter of personal discernment. Each person must be at peace with the lifestyle he or she supports.

*Abundance*: Once the tithe and basic provisions have been secured, you may have excess money. This is called abundance. What you do with the abundance is a direct reflection of your heart. You can spend it on selfish desires or on godly enhancements to your purpose in life. This is not to say you should never spend it on your pleasure. God generously gives us gifts and wants us to enjoy His creation. It may be His will that you simply enjoy His blessings as a means of building your intimacy with Him. He may also want you to invest the abundance on tools to build relationships with others. This requires some discernment of His personal will for your life. Family vacations, club memberships, expensive dinners, etc., are neither godly nor ungodly by themselves. But your purpose in making those purchases can be. Using the money on things that are not kingdom-related is called spending. Once you've used it, it's gone. Using it on kingdom-building purchases is investing; there will be eternal dividends in God's kingdom. Sometimes there's a fine line between the two, but God knows the heart. And if we're honest, we usually do too.

*Offerings*: Another way to invest your abundance is in the form of an offering. An offering, like a tithe, is given directly to God's kingdom work through support of your local church or another ministry. But an offer-

> **Money is a tool to be used to carry out God's will. Its four purposes are: tithing, provisions, offerings and abundance.**

ing is different from a tithe because it isn't an obligation. Instead, it's a free-will gesture that reflects a heart's desire to see God glorified in this life and His kingdom fully realized in the next.

The Bible mandates that we share with the needy—widows, orphans, and the poor. Offerings can be given over and above your tithes when you learn of opportunities to help meet special needs. Some offerings may need to be spontaneous, in order to be an accurate expression of your heart. But having a strategy for making offerings should be included in your financial blueprint.

## STRATEGIES FOR YOUR MONEY

Knowing the different uses of money, let's begin to generate some ideas for how you want to approach each category.

*Personal strategies for tithing*: Tithing from your income means committing 10 percent off the top. Some people interpret this as 10 percent of net, others as 10 percent of gross. And it has been suggested that your decision be based on the type of blessing you want from God—a net blessing or gross! Either way, God has promised to bless the tithe. Malachi 3:10 says, "Test me in this . . . and see if I will not throw open the floodgates of heaven and pour out so much blessing that you will not have room enough for it." You cannot out-give to God. He always gives back more in return—not necessarily more money, but always more blessings, whether in intimacy with Him, joy, spiritual maturity, health, and so on. And sometimes He gives back money too. This doesn't mean you should view God as a slot machine—giving in order to receive. But you can be confident that any amount of giving with the right motives, no matter how little, will have a great return.

> **You cannot out-give God. He always gives back more in return—not necessarily more money, but always more blessings**

*Personal strategies for provisions*: The most important thing to determine for your provisions is the standard of living, or lifestyle, you will pursue. Without a plan, most people tend to set lifestyle according to their present salary. As the rewards of work grow, so does the standard of living. But living strategically for God means using foresight. Your provisions are simply a means to an end. And you should have a standard of living in mind—along with a budget—for each stage of life along the way. The first place to start is with a current budget. Do you know where all your money is going right now? Do you track your spending regularly to keep it in line with your budget plan? For future budgets, you can project most everyday expenses for the lifestyle you will pursue.

In addition, getting out of debt, paying off a home mortgage, funding college education, and saving for retirement are things to include when planning for your provisions. Do you have a strategy for saying, "Enough is enough?" Is there a standard of living at which, once achieved, you will begin to commit excess funds to saving or more giving? Should you consider a goal for financial autonomy? At what age would you like your investments to support you? At retirement? Or perhaps earlier so you can be free to serve God's kingdom in additional ways? Do you have goals for your net worth? How much do you want to accumulate by age 30 . . . 40 . . . 50. . . 60? Another consideration is the risk/reward for your investment plan . . . how conservative or risky should you be at each stage of life? Once

> **Is there a standard of living at which, once achieved, you will begin to commit excess funds to saving or more giving?**

your provision goals are thought out, you should weigh them against your earning opportunities. You may need to pray for additional financial blessings. Or you may need to change your career or your financial goals.

*Personal strategies for abundance*: How will you use any excess funds you receive? Will you simply plow it back into your ever-expanding standard of living? Or do you have a plan for achieving other goals? How much will you allot for personal ministry dreams? How much for relationship-building experiences with your spouse, your family, your un-churched friends? Are there any personal accomplishments you hope to realize that might require a financial investment? Are there any personal pleasures you will grant yourself as part of your strategy? Your plan for abundance should also include your goals for kingdom building. Perhaps you would determine a percentage of abundance that will go to the church and a percentage you will spend on yourself. Listen to the pure desires of your heart and define the blueprint for your extra finances.

*Personal strategies for offerings*: Offerings are your opportunity to express a heart of gratitude to God and a commitment to see His kingdom reign. Free-will gifts demonstrate something different than those that are required. How you seize these opportunities says a lot about you. God gives us talents, positions of authority, relationships, and finances to do with as we choose. When we voluntarily use them to glorify God, it proclaims Him a priority. The first commandment calls us to have no other gods before Him. Offerings allow us to live out the first commandment in a very tangible way. They show that we are not using our money to serve ourselves or someone else. They are presented directly to God as a sacrifice.

> **We were designed for generosity. Giving may seem like an obligation to many, but to us it's a great opportunity.**

We were designed for generosity. Giving may seem like an obligation to many, but to us it's a great opportunity. Jesus said that it's more blessed to give than to receive (Acts 20:35), and Paul wrote that God loves a cheerful giver (2 Corinthians 9:7). When we are generous . . .

1.  We demonstrate the nature of God, who is more generous than anyone. We were made in His image, so we were designed to reflect His character, including His generosity.

2.  We experience the joy of being used by God as an instrument of His goodness. Our lives are fuller and more enriching when God's resources flow through us and we can see Him meet people's needs.

3.  We break ourselves of materialism. A materialistic attitude, a relentless temptation in our culture, takes us in spiritually harmful directions and can choke the fruitfulness of God's work in our lives. Giving destroys the power of whatever hold materialism has on us.

4.  We invest in God's kingdom and lay up treasures in heaven. God's word tells us that even the simplest act of giving a cup of cold water to one who is thirsty will with it receive a reward in heaven.

It only makes sense that if God is a sacrificial, generous giver, and if He's putting His nature within us as we grow to be like Him, then we will be sacrificial, generous givers too. Those who learn to give away much of what God has given them experience the fullness of His joy in ways that many other people don't. This is a spiritual secret that many people have never understood, a profound key to the ways of God's kingdom. Liberal giving is inextricably connected with spiritual maturity and joy.

When you consider your blueprint for your life, what kind of giver do you want to be in the end? At the end of your life, how much do you want to have spent supporting the poor? How much do you want to invest in kingdom-building? You can be spontaneous about how and when and where you give—spontaneity is where much of the joy comes from—but you should have a strategy (and perhaps a dedicated budget) for making offerings that reflects your views of life and God's will. Moreover, you should plan your giving with an eternal perspective. In light of eternity, each of us has been given a little bit of time and a little bit of opportunity to invest what is temporary and decaying to receive what is of unlimited everlasting value.

> **Money fuels your mission from God.**

## How Much Is Enough?

The most important question you can ask regarding your finances is, "How much is enough?" In asking this question, you will learn two things. First, it will help you to anticipate the amount you will need to support your life goals. Second, it will show you where to draw the line when your wealth begins to exceed your current lifestyle.

The first time you calculate your spending needs for your entire lifetime, it may be eye-opening. The costs of housing, transportation, food, college expenses, weddings, vacations, and retirement add up. By putting a number on the price tag of life, you will be able to envision the income requirements for funding your life blueprint.

In addition, counting the cost enables you to recognize when it's time to give away your excess to God's kingdom. God gives us more than we need so we'll have something to give to others and to invest in His kingdom. Many people fall into the trap of raising their lifestyle every time their income goes up, and they never have enough to be as generous as they want to be. There's very little margin between their lifestyle costs and their actual income. Or worse yet, their lifestyle costs exceed their income, and debt begins to rise steadily. If you don't count the cost and set a spending figure ahead of time, you may fall into this trap of raising your lifestyle every time your income goes up. Lifestyle changes should be planned as a proactive part of your blueprint, not a reactionary decision to an unexpected raise or windfall.

## Discovering the Financial Life You Were Born to Live

Setting goals for your finances may come much more easily than for other, less tangible areas of your life, simply because the nature of money allows you to include very concrete steps and objectives. You will be able to measure your progress much more specifically than you can with your spiritual growth or relationships. As you set your goals for your financial blueprint, remember that you are a steward of God's resources, not

> As you set your goals for your financial blueprint, remember that you are a steward of God's resources, not an owner of your resources. Fix your gaze firmly on eternity, ordering your priorities around what truly matters.

an owner of your resources. Fix your gaze firmly on eternity, ordering your priorities around what truly matters. Always remember that the money you manage can either be spent on temporary pleasures or be leveraged for eternal gain. God wants you to be blessed financial and enjoy His gifts, but His greater goal for your finances is for you to make investments in His kingdom work, where the benefits last forever.

# BLUEPRINT FOR *Life*

*Chapter Eleven*

---

# Your Career Blueprint

*"But more than anything else, put God's work first and do what He wants.
Then the other things will be yours as well."*

*~ Matthew 6:33*

People's feelings about work run the gamut of attitudes and emotions. Some love what they do. Others loathe the idea of work completely and daydream about winning the lottery so they'll never have to work again. We hear this sentiment often in the songs and expressions of pop culture: "Take this job and shove it, I ain't working here no more"; "I don't want to work, I just want to bang on the drum all day"; "I'm taking what they're giving cause I'm working for a living"; "That ain't working . . . that's the way you do it . . . you play the guitar on the MTV . . . money for nothing and your chicks for free"; "I owe, I owe . . . it's off to work I go." Clearly, many people don't feel very positive about their job.

Not everything you hear is so pessimistic though. There are tributes to faithful work as well: "Hello West Virginia coal miner, let me thank you for your time, you work a forty hour week for a living, just to send it on down the line." In a time of high unemployment, appreciation for a regular paycheck rises dramatically. Some people really do love their job, while some blur the lines between love and addiction, working constantly because it keeps them busy or masks other issues in their lives. And some vacillate between enthusiasm and dread, finding fulfillment one week and dreading Monday morning the next. As a culture, we seem to have a love/ hate relationship with our work.

So what's your attitude about work? Does it alternate between extremes? Are you mostly content? Or do you long for a day when you can retire independently wealthy and put it all behind you? More importantly, what does God think about work? Is it a punishment for sinners? Adam's curse? Part of living in a fallen world? Does He even care about your daily grind, or is He too busy tracking your church attendance? Does God have an opinion about work at all?

## Hi ho, hi ho . . .

This may come as a surprise, but God had work in mind from the very beginning. When He first created Adam, "The Lord God took the man and put him in the Garden of Eden to work it

> **God had work in mind from the very beginning.**

and take care of it" (Genesis 2:15 NIV). According to this passage, one of the first things God did with His climactic creation was to place him in the garden for a specific purpose—not just to enjoy the garden, not to eat the fruit, not only to walk and talk with God, but also to "work it and take care of it." Work was not part of Adam's punishment. True, work became toilsome after he was banished from the garden for eating from the tree of life. In explaining the consequences of their sin, God said, "Because you listened to your wife and ate the fruit when I told you not to, I have placed a curse upon the soil. All your life you will struggle to extract a living from it. It will grow thorns and thistles for you, and you shall eat its grasses. All your life you will sweat to master it, until your dying day" (Genesis 3:17-19 TLB). So Adam's sin certainly changed the nature of earthly work. But it didn't change the basic concept that work is one of our inherent responsibilities. Fall or no fall, our work was part of the plan from the start. And it was meant to be pleasing to God.

If your main career goal is to reach a point where you can retire to a life of leisure . . . if work is just something you suffer through to get to the rest of your life . . . if it's anything less than a channel for using your life to bring glory to God . . . then perhaps you should take a deeper look at why God invented work.

> **God has a plan for your life's work. And He means for your career to dovetail perfectly with your purpose in life.**

God has a plan for your life's work. And He means for your career to dovetail perfectly with your purpose in life. When it does, your job will support and serve your overall Blueprint for Life. God's plan is based on maximizing your fulfillment in serving His purpose for your life.

In stark contrast, the culture has a plan for your career as well. This plan is based primarily on maximizing things like income, recognition, and freedom. When those are your goals, you may notice a tension between your current career path and the one God is calling you to pursue. There may be an underlying sense that work was meant to be something more.

There is a default track in this world that people often mistake for God's will—we go to school, we continue with college, we seek a job, we plan for retirement . . . those are the stages of life many of us expect to go through. On this track, success is defined by maximum achievement, maximum income, and maximum recognition. Without realizing it, many people live institutional lives because they never stop to think outside this box. As long as we do our best, we think God is pleased. But God doesn't want us to do our best at just anything. He wants us to our best at *His* thing. Remember, Ephesians 2:10 explains that God created specific "good works" for us to accomplish in our lifetime. And only when we are careful to discover and complete those works will we find satisfaction.

> **But God doesn't want us to do our best at just anything. He wants us to our best at His thing.**

In Jeremiah, God says, "You will seek me and find me when you seek me with all your heart" (Jeremiah 29:13 NIV) Career accomplishments, apart from our purpose in life, were never meant to bring long-term fulfillment.

Instead of asking, "Does my career choice fulfill my maximum earning potential?" we should ask, "Does my career choice allow me to leverage my skills and talents to pursue God's purpose for my life?" He doesn't always lead us to the highest paying job. He leads us to the opportunities for greatest fruitfulness. When deciding between two employment options, the one with the best retirement plan, vacation allowance, and other benefits may not be the one that lines up with our purpose. If we focus on provision alone, we may miss our mission. But if we focus on fulfilling our mission, the provision for that mission will follow.

## THE THIRD PLATFORM

Like money, your career is a tool that should be used to help you serve God with your whole life. Just as your family and your church community are platforms for service, your career should also be viewed as a platform for carrying out God's work. Sometimes it's primarily a financial vehicle to fund the other areas of your life. Sometimes it's the primary vehicle

> **Your career should be viewed as a platform for carrying out God's work.**

through which you exercise your God-given mission in life. Most often, it's a combination of both.

Your work should never be your reason for living. Serving God is. Similarly, serving yourself should never be your reason for working. Serving God should. If your driving ambition for going to work each day is to get ahead financially or to experience the thrill of unraveling the latest challenge or to just make it to the weekend—anything other than glorifying your Creator—then you could be missing the whole point God had in mind when He invented work.

When it comes to designing a Blueprint for Life, your career goals must be in alignment with your other goals. Many people don't set their career goals high enough. They settle for whatever employment they can find. As a result, their job can end up dictating their lives and limiting their other goals. Because most jobs require some kind of experience, they feel like they must continue to pursue the career track they settled for because that's where their experience is. They often feel trapped by circumstances and unable to pursue their real God-given passions. Even when they know they are called to something different, they are enslaved by the reality that bills and debts have to be paid. They have found it difficult to step into what God has really called them to do.

Other people are so devoted to their careers that the other areas of life suffer. One of the most common traps is to get so wrapped up in work that they have very little time for God and family. There are several reasons people become so vulnerable to this trap: because career and purpose are so closely related, they justify devoting extra hours to "fulfilling God's calling" even at the expense of time with family; there can be immediate consequences to sacrificing time at work, while the damage to relationships at home is much more subtle; satisfying the desire to achieve is more tangible at work than it is at home; and so on. But God will never put us in a position of consistently and persistently stealing time from our most meaningful relationships in order to accomplish career goals. There may be brief seasons when this happens—a pressing deadline, an unusually demanding travel schedule, etc.—but if it's an ongoing dynamic, there's a problem. If you find this to be an issue in your life, you should pursue God about your career until your career goals complement your life's overall mission statement—including your goals and priorities for relationships. Your calling in life should drive your career, not vice versa. The bottom line is that your career needs to enable your overall life blueprint instead of undermining it.

> **God will never put us in a position of consistently and persistently stealing time from our most meaningful relationships in order to accomplish career goals.**

## THE PURPOSES OF WORK—PROVISION AND PASSION

On average, a person spends about one-third of his or her waking life at work. That's more time than is consumed by any other single activity in a person's life. To plod along through life without a plan for this area seems careless at best. But before you can develop a plan for your work, it helps to understand the purposes work serves.

First, we work to provide income for our basic economic necessities; to buy food, clothing, shelter, and other needs. Second, we work to experience fulfillment through the exercising of our gifts, talents, and personal

> **Your calling in life should drive your career, not vice versa.**

passions. In other words, we work first because we have to, and second because we want to. For some, a career enables their calling in life by providing an income along the way. For others, a career *is* their calling in life, allowing them a direct avenue for exercising their God-given talents.

It's important to realize this—that your career may not necessarily be the same as your purpose. It may just play a supporting role in your overall purpose. Even if you feel called to do ministry, you need to be able to think of ministry in non-traditional ways. Few people are called to do ministry professionally within the context of a local church or ministry organization. But all professions have opportunities for ministry through the relationships and activities involved with them. You can view your work—and really every area of life—as an opportunity to minister to others. If your job is staying at home caring for children or other family members—you too have vital work that God has purposed for your life. So your career blueprint is relevant not only to a formal career with a paycheck but also to any role you occupy or any vocation you choose to pursue in the home or at church or in community service. In addition, if your role may be to somehow support someone else in your household who has a specific career, your blueprint may relate to how to be a good steward as you serve and support them.

Regardless, whatever we do for a vocation or as employment, we do it because we have needs for provision and we have a need to find fulfillment in our work. These are our two primary motivations.

## FROM PROVISION TO PASSION TO PURPOSE

There are many philosophies as to how these two motives—provision and passion—should be balanced. Books, essays, and seminars have been produced to address this ageless conflict. Some proclaim, "Do what you enjoy, the money will follow." Others suggest you build a nest egg for early retirement, and then pursue your passions in life.

Blueprint for Life goes a step further. A thorough career blueprint should be based on the concept of moving from provision, to passion, to purpose. Provision alone is not enough to sustain career

> **A thorough career blueprint should be based on the concept of moving from provision, to passion, to purpose.**

satisfaction. But neither is passion because it's possible to become passionate about something that isn't part of your purpose in life. And if your career energy goes toward anything that isn't your calling in life, you will end up cheated out of the fulfillment God meant for you to experience.

Early on, most people must consider the pure utilitarian role of work—to provide income. But over time, the ideal career path will take you toward a situation where your career directly fulfills your God-given purpose. This isn't the case for every individual. But for anyone who works outside the home, it's a dynamic that should be taken into consideration. If you neglect the need for provision, your ship will run aground. But if you neglect the need to fulfill your purpose, then your ship never truly leaves the harbor at all.

## When I Grow Up . . .

### Provision

You work because you have to. Earning an income is necessary for your basic economic needs. But provision alone is not enough to sustain career satisfaction.

### Passion

You work because you want to. You crave fulfillment through the exercising of your gifts, talents, and personal passions. Passion also is not enough to sustain satisfaction. It is also possible to become passionate about something that isn't part of your purpose, and you will miss the sense of fulfillment God created you for.

### Purpose

You work because you are called to. This is how you fulfill your God-given life purpose and calling. In the case of those who work outside the home, consider that over time, an idea career path will take you toward a situation where your career directly fulfills your God-given purpose. For some, a career enables their calling in life by providing income. For others, a career is their calling in life.

In our culture, the number one substitute for a fulfilling career is the career based on financial gain. You may begin your career with the simple, honest objective of providing a living for yourself and your family. But little by little, you may begin to see the awesome power of work to provide. If a little work affords you the basic needs, then a lot of work should mean abundance and luxury, right? Before you realize it, you find yourself on a treadmill, chasing work as a means of feeding an appetite for possessions. Is that part of a life blueprint for your career? Not likely.

As one writer observed, "Why is the idea of working less such a heresy to Americans? Probably because we are caught in a larger web of wants, desires, and assumptions that conflict with the desire for leisure time. In simpler terms, we work to spend and we don't know how to stop." *(S.J. Power, 1994)*

It's tempting to think that we should approach our careers with reckless emphasis on passion and gratification. Certainly the money will follow, right? But not everyone experiences instant fame and fortune by playing their favorite game. Should everyone who enjoys golf quit his job to join the PGA tour? Should every enjoyable hobby turn into an income generator? That isn't realistic or even possible. It's true that we should follow our God-given passions, but we shouldn't be reckless about deciding what those passions are or assume that because we have them, we are therefore to earn our living exclusively from them.

Clearly, a balanced plan is the best strategy. When you get right down to it, there are some very practical questions to ask. Do you need your career to provide a salary? Then you should plan for that. Can you find paying work that exercises your unique skills and talents? Then you should pursue it. Is your spending under control, enabling you maximum freedom as you consider your career options? Are there non-career activities that might serve as an alternative outlet for your personal passions, freeing you up to make objective decisions about your employment?

In the end, God wants us to learn one thing from our work: that He and He alone meets our needs. He is our provider, blessing our work and causing it to bear fruit. And He wants to be our passion, giving us fulfillment as we use our skills and talents to fulfill our purpose in this life.

> **Blueprint for Life focuses on determining the "non-negotiables" of your life blueprint; then build your career goals around those.**

## ZERO-BASED CAREER PLANNING

So how should you set goals for your career? Culture urges us to prioritize money and fame first; then, once those goals are met, we can pursue the other things that are important to us. Instead, Blueprint for Life focuses on determining the "non-negotiables" of your life blueprint; then build your career goals around those. This approach is called "zero-based career planning." It starts with zero career mandates and builds your ideal career based on the non-negotiables that you have determined must be in place in order to serve your purpose in life.

For example, you may decide that your overall purpose in life requires that you live in a certain city. Your extended family is there, your aging parents are there, and the church that God is using to feed you spiritually is there. Living in that city is a non-negotiable. So right away, you can rule out all jobs that would require you to move away. That's how zero-based career planning works.

Other non-negotiables might include: number of days willing to travel, salary minimum, nature of work, moral or ethical standards upheld, opportunity to exercise core skills and talents, etc. Once you define your career non-negotiables, it's much easier to evaluate the different job opportunities available to you.

In particular, there are three key areas to consider for zero-based career planning:

*Calling*: The first question to ask is, "What am I called to do?" Your calling is your unique contribution to build God's kingdom during your lifetime. The Bible is filled with stories of people who were approached by God with a specific task or mission to accomplish with their lives. It's possible that God's will for your life can also be described this way. Has God put a calling in your heart that might involve using your career platform as its foundation? Is there a certain kind of work you feel called to perform during your lifetime? Are there any strengths, weaknesses, or overwhelming desires that might suggest some particular areas you should focus in on—or some you should avoid? Does your life's mission statement involve specific goals that are related to professional accomplishments?

Along those lines, if you could be anything God called you to be professionally, what would it be? Can you identify some logical "stepping stones" to take you from where you are to your ultimate career destination? What would be the next step in that progression?

*Earning*: The second question to ask is, "What am I called to earn?" Perhaps you don't identify with any one occupational calling in particular. Maybe the best way for you to fulfill your life's mission statement is simply to use your career opportunities to fund the areas of life you're genuinely passionate about. It could be your heart's desire simply to give money to various ministry needs as they arise, or to be financially free to spend liberal amounts of time with your children . . . your spouse . . . or volunteering in ministry. Whether directly or indirectly, your career can fund your passions.

If you could achieve anything God called you to achieve financially, what would it be? What kind of earnings would it take for you to realize that goal? It might be a large figure, or it might mean simply working diligently and spending wisely to afford you the time and money to pursue your dreams. Will your current career path allow you to answer God's call? Is your greatest career need just to remain diligent in what you're already doing? Or will you need to make some adjustments—perhaps a complete overhaul of your career to arrive at your long-term earnings goals? Can you identify any stepping stones between where you are and where you'd like to be? What's the next logical step for you at this point?

> **People tend to be pretty good at knowing what they're chasing vocationally, but pretty lousy at realizing what it's costing them along the way.**

*Time*: Finally, you should consider how much time you plan to spend at work. This sounds simple, but it's something few people really consider. Almost everyone can name an ultimate job description or a salary range that they hope to accomplish one day. But not many people think in terms of how much they're willing to pay for those goals in terms of their time. As a result, people tend to be pretty good at knowing what they're chasing vocationally, but pretty lousy at realizing what it's costing them along the way.

Relationships take time. Contemplating life and making plans takes time. Recharging your batteries takes time. Pausing to put life in perspective takes time. Are there any non-negotiables that you would name for how you spend your time? Are there limits to how much time you're willing to invest in your career before you say, "Enough!"? The Bible commands us to rest one day a week. What about the other days? How many hours should you allot to accomplish your career objectives? Eight hours? Ten? Twelve? How much time should you set aside for everything else? Are you prepared to guard that time with all vigilance? Throughout your career, will you allow more time for work, or less? You need a strategy for placing limits on your work time. Otherwise, it will take on a life of its own and encroach on your other personal goals.

The 80/20 rule states that 20 percent of your time generates 80 percent of your results. If you are strategic in your use of time—focusing on the 20 percent and delegating or eliminating the 80 percent—you can increase your impact while reducing your effort.

## DISCOVERING THE CAREER YOU WERE BORN TO ENJOY

We have purposely saved the area of career for last—not because it's the least important but because in our culture there's a tendency to think it's the most important. From early in school, there is a strong emphasis on career goals: "What do you want to be when you grow up?" As a result, there's more of a struggle to keep this area in balance than with any other category we've examined. We hope to make a point by discussing

> **Career accomplishments are extremely important, but they must be balanced within a comprehensive blueprint that takes all other life goals into consideration.**

this area last. Career accomplishments are extremely important, but they must be balanced within a comprehensive blueprint that takes all other life goals into consideration. The career component should simply facilitate or enable the overall life blueprint. It should never become the ever-urgent center of it.

As you develop specific goals for your career, seek balance between a reckless pursuit of your passions, on one hand, and feeling stuck in your current path, on the other. As much as you can at this point in time, determine your overall purpose. Then eliminate steps that distract from your purpose or lead you away from it. Realize that God sometimes takes us on unexpected detours—to Him they aren't really detours at all, but they appear that way to us. If that happens, don't be alarmed. But as far as it's up to you in the choices He gives you, choose the directions you know to be consistent with your purpose.

BLUEPRINT
FOR •
L*i*FE.

*Chapter Twelve*

# View from the Porch Swing

"…but I focus on this one thing: forgetting the past and looking forward to what lies ahead, I press on to reach the end of the race and receive the heavenly prize for which God, through Christ Jesus, is calling us."

*~ Philippians 3:13b–14*

Very few people look back at the end of their lives and have no regrets. Most of us wish we had done some things we didn't do, or that we hadn't done some of the things we did do. We wish we had invested our lives more intentionally, more wisely, more meaningfully. We wanted our lives to have as much impact as possible.

If we can see with that perspective—if we can know that one day, we're likely to look back and regret what we should have done differently—then why don't we go ahead and do things differently now? Why don't we choose to plan for the sense of satisfaction we want to have then? Why don't we do whatever is necessary to live without regrets? The truth is… we can. We can have that "looking back" perspective even as we're looking ahead to the rest of our lives.

## LOOKING BACK AT THE BIG FIVE

Over the last five chapters, you've taken a close look at five areas of your life that will require an intentional approach if you want to fulfill your God-given purpose and live with balance. As you've explored these "Big Five" areas in detail, you have some big questions to consider: Do you have a plan to make your life count? Are you living with intentionality or are you drifting along, accepting whatever life brings your way? Are you confident that when you arrive at the end of your life, you'll have accomplished the mission God sent you to accomplish? In other words, will you have aligned your passions and gifts

> **Are you living with intentionality or are you drifting along, accepting whatever life brings your way?**

with God's purposes in order to bring Him glory? These are vital questions to answer as you seek to fulfill your mission in life. .

If you're like most people, you'll tend to answer these questions in light of your highest priorities—those areas of life that seem most relevant and most pressing to your personal fulfillment. But be sure to apply *each* of the five areas of your life, not just one or two. At the end of your days, will your relationship with God have been the foundation of everything else you do? Will you have grown to the spiritual depth both you and He desire? Will you have lived a life of balance, nurturing the relationships He entrusted you with? Will you have been a trustworthy steward of the financial resources you were responsible for? Will you be able to look back on your life—every aspect of it—with satisfaction that you completed all you were given to do? Wrestling with these questions—really taking time to answer them thoughtfully—can help you discern how to take the next steps toward living without regrets.

Near the end of chapter 5, you walked through an exercise of imagining yourself sitting on a porch swing looking back over your life. In that exercise, you looked at all your future dreams and put them into the past tense, listing all the things you will have done. You envisioned your most significant, non-negotiable goals—things that would cause you serious regret if

> **Will you be able to look back on your life—every aspect of it—with satisfaction that you completed all you were given to do?**

left undone. For most people, this comes out as statements like, "I had a long and satisfying career in the field of education and impacted the lives of many students." Or, "I instilled godly values in my children and gave them the spiritual foundation they needed." The possibilities for these statements are nearly limitless, so you likely came up with quite a few that were uniquely tailored to your dreams for your life and the gifts and passions that God has given you.

But that was before we looked closely at the five areas of your life. Now that you have gone through the last five chapters, have those statements changed at all? Perhaps your earlier version of this exercise emphasized career and financial goals and only generally addressed spiritual and relational issues—or vice versa. The questions raised in the five area-specific chapters may have helped you refine your goals. Take some time to think through this porch-swing exercise again, reviewing the life you will have lived if you intentionally pursue your purpose.

As you reflect back on the years when you were young and single, in the prime of your career, and in all the other phases of your life . . .

- Will you smile as you remember the ways you pursued life with an adventurous spirit, squeezing everything you could out of it?

- Will you have found your perfect soul mate to partner with on a joyous journey of creating a family?

- Will you know that you fully poured yourself into your children, cultivated precious memories with them, and seized every moment that you could to show them your love?

• Will you have a sense of peace about making the most of your career? Will you feel confident that you leveraged it as a platform for your God-given purpose?

• Will you be satisfied about being wise and disciplined to keep your priorities straight, putting God first, human relationships second, and career third?

• Did you have an intentional strategy to maximize your relationships?

• Will your "impact" remain? Will your accomplishments live long after you breathe your last breath?

• What treasures will be awaiting you in eternity? Did you spend your life sending treasures on ahead to your eternal dwelling place, or did you simply consume all that you could only to leave the rest behind?

> **Did you spend your life sending treasures on ahead to your eternal dwelling place, or did you simply consume all that you could only to leave the rest behind?**

These are only some of the many questions you can ask—you could look back over your life from many different angles—but it's important to go through this kind of exercise. Why? Because it shifts your perspective. It prompts you not to think in the short term or to live reactively to whatever comes your way, but to go ahead and plan for the long view. In fact, these questions really emphasize the longest view possible—eternity.

## Looking Back, Looking Forward

While you're spending time looking back on life from your imaginary porch swing, take some time to look ahead too. Will you be excited about what lies ahead or nervous about what awaits you? Will your regrets about the past color your perceptions of the future? If you have received Jesus as your Savior, eternity will be absolutely amazing and fulfilling. You can count on that. But will you wish that you had given more thought to your eternal rewards earlier in life, when you could plan your investments of time, talent, and treasure in God's kingdom? If you have fully accomplished what God has equipped you to do, and done so with excellence, you will have a great reward awaiting you in heaven. He promised.

We saw earlier how scripture repeatedly urges us to live with this reward in mind. Though many people think it's unspiritual to be motivated by rewards, Jesus encouraged His disciples often by talking about the rewards they would receive for their sacrifices, their giving, their service, their suffering, and more. He continually directed their focus away from immediate benefits and toward the eternal benefits of following Him. If God's direction for our lives only emphasized the relatively tiny next few decades and neglected the infinite existence we will experience afterward, we really couldn't say He was looking out for our best interests. But He is, of course. God's Word is always reminding us of the big picture and lifting our vision beyond our immediate circumstances. He wants the best for us, not just now but forever. If we want to experience His best, we'll need to live with this view from the porch swing in mind.

While you're sitting on that swing in your mind's eye, imagine Jesus appearing in front of you—just materializing out of thin air. You can look into His eyes. You can even reach out and touch Him if you want to. And you can talk to Him and hear Him speak to you. Now imagine the conversation you might have with Him, once you've gotten over the shock of seeing Him, about His plans for your "forever." Imagine Him reviewing each stage of your life and each of the five areas at each stage, explaining how your decisions have impacted the eternity you're about to face. Hear Him recount all of the times you

> **While you're sitting on that swing in your mind's eye, imagine Jesus appearing in front of you—just materializing out of thin air.**

gave sacrificially to His work, of all the times you invested your time in someone who needed to experience His touch through you, of all the opportunities you had to be completely self-serving and decided instead to give of yourself to others, and of all the times you chose to worship Him and pray for His kingdom in spite of the difficulties you were going through. He points out every example of your right priorities: those times when you put Him above your own agenda, your family and friends above your work, the purpose of your work above the distractions from it, and on and on. Deep down, you realize there were many more opportunities to do even more of these things, but He doesn't mention them because He's too gracious and merciful. He has come to encourage you, not to burden you with guilt. But even in His encouragement, you realize how much He values the ways you've invested your life—and how He plans to reward you for them. You start to wonder how much greater the rewards would have been if only . . ., and then your mind goes to everything that could possibly fill in that blank. And you deeply long for an opportunity to turn back the clock and do even more.

Now come back to the present time, while you have many years left to live, and begin developing your Blueprint for Life out of that sense of

> **You don't have to wait until heaven to live with an eternal perspective. Eternity is already a reality in your life.**

longing. Let that hunger to serve God, to live with meaning and purpose, and to plan for eternity drive you to set concrete, reachable goals that cover every area of your life and will one day lead to a satisfying view from the porch swing—and a satisfying conversation with Jesus. You don't have to wait until heaven to live with an eternal perspective. Eternity is already a reality in your life. There's no reason not to go ahead and ground your life with that eternal perspective in mind.

## TAKING THE NEXT STEP

Do you have a strategy for doing that? This book has been one step toward developing that strategy, but if you're like most people, thinking this way is the exception, not the rule. If you don't have a Blueprint for Life, you may end up with a lot of regrets. You may close out the last chapter of your life having missed far more opportunities than you took advantage of. You may wish for a do-over, but God gives us only one lifetime to get it right. He is very gracious to help us make up for lost time when we get started late, of course, but He doesn't turn back the clock. Each day is an opportunity to either leverage time for eternity or spend it wastefully on things that don't last. When you have a strategy, you can maximize that opportunity. You can wake up each morning with a sense of adventure about how you'll use the next 16 hours for God's eternal purposes. Having a blueprint will ensure that you can make an incremental deposit into your eternal account every single day. And as you pursue the purpose God created you to fulfill, you will discover the life you were born to live.

Developing a strategy isn't a one-time event. It's an ongoing process. We encourage you now to take the next step in pursuing your purpose and calling by designing your own Blueprint for Life. The book you have just read was inspired by the ground breaking Blueprint for Life study curriculum. The Blueprint for Life study was introduced several years ago and since then, over 20,000 people have been impacted by this life changing study. There is more information in the back of this book about the Blueprint for Life study.

> **Each day is an opportunity to either leverage time for eternity or spend it wastefully on things that don't last.**

The Blueprint for Life study will guide you through the five areas of your life and help you define your goals in each of them. By the end of the study, you will be living with a sense of direction and purpose, confident that your gifts and passions are integral parts of your design. And you'll be well on your way toward accomplishing God's purposes for your life for His glory.

A clear purpose and plan along with the courage to follow through provides you the opportunity to end your life with deep satisfaction saying, "I did it. I succeeded. I lived the life I was born to live."

Life is epic when you have a Blueprint for Life!

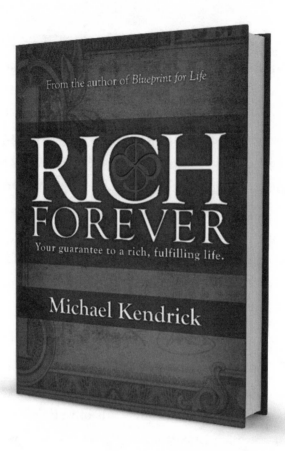

# If you've always dreamed of becoming rich,
## *forever is the time to do it.*

Join author Michael Kendrick on his journey of making tens of millions of dollars, losing them, then making even more again. You will learn life changing principles that will help you succeed and possibly even become wealthy in the process. More importantly, you will learn how to amass the kind of wealth that lasts *forever*.

For more information or to purchase,
please visit richforever.com.

# ABOUT MIKE KENDRICK

Michael Kendrick is co-founder and Senior Partner of his Atlanta-based private equity firm, Roswell Capital Partners, LLC. As an investment banker, Michael has raised or made equity commitments in excess of a billion dollars in private equity financing for over 170 public companies. He has used the knowledge gained in his business career as a catalyst for founding, developing and funding organizations dedicated to impacting the world for Christ. In addition to starting the Blueprint for Life organization, Michael is founder of Ministry Ventures, a non-profit organization dedicated to launching new Christian ministries. Since its inception, Ministry Ventures has been instrumental in launching over 40 new Christian non-profit organizations. Michael is a founding member and former elder of North Point Community Church. Michael holds a Masters Degree in Business Administration from Embry Riddle University and a Bachelors Degree with honors in Aerospace Engineering from Auburn University. Michael and his wife, Michele, reside in Alpharetta, Georgia with their two sons and one daughter.

# ABOUT BEN ORTLIP

Ben Ortlip began his writing career in the advertising industry in the 1980s, where his fresh writing style in television, radio and print won numerous prestigious awards. Eventually his heart for ministry led him to his true calling, where he has been the writing partner of several prominent Christian authors. In addition to writing books, scripts, and study curriculum, Ben is a seasoned film director and executive producer, having overseen projects for Campus Crusade for Christ, Injoy, FamilyLife, Walk Thru The Bible, North Point Ministries, and dozens of other trend-setting ministries. Ben is the co-author of the Blueprint for Life curriculum. He and his wife Lisa, live in Cumming, Georgia with their eight children.